Printed in the United States of America

Composition by Graphic World
Printing/Binding by Banta Book Group

StayWell
780 Township Line Rd.
Yardley, PA 19067

ISBN 1-58480-341-X

08 09 10 11 / 9 8 7 6 5

TABLE OF CONTENTS

HEALTH PRECAUTIONS AND GUIDELINES DURING TRAINING

The American Red Cross has trained millions of people in first aid and cardiopulmonary resuscitation (CPR) using manikins as training aids.

The Red Cross follows widely accepted guidelines for cleaning and decontaminating training manikins. **If these guidelines are adhered to, the risk of any kind of disease transmission during training is extremely low.**

To help minimize the risk of disease transmission, you should follow some basic health precautions and guidelines while participating in training. You should take precautions if you have a condition that would increase your risk or other participants' risk of exposure to infections. Request a separate training manikin if you—

- Have an acute condition, such as a cold a sore throat, or cuts or sores on the hands or around your mouth.
- Know you are seropositive (have had a positive blood test) for hepatitis B surface antigen (HBsAg), indicating that you are currently infected with the hepatitis B virus.*
- Know you have a chronic infection indicated by long-term seropositivity (long-term positive blood tests) for the HBsAg* or a positive blood test for anti-human immunodeficiency virus (HIV) [that is, a positive test for antibodies to HIV, the virus that causes many severe infections including acquired immunodeficiency syndrome (AIDS)].
- Have had a positive blood test for hepatitis C.
- Have a condition that makes you unusually likely to get an infection.

To obtain information about testing for individual health status, visit the CDC Web site at **www.cdc.gov/ncidod/diseases/hepatitis/c/faq.htm.**

If you decide you should have your own manikin, ask your instructor if he or she can provide one for you to use. You will not be asked to explain why in your request. The manikin will not be used by anyone else until it has been cleaned according to the recommended end-of-class decontamination procedures. Because the number of manikins available for class use is limited, the more advance notice you give, the more likely it is that you can be provided a separate manikin.

GUIDELINES

In addition to taking the precautions regarding manikins, you can further protect yourself and other participants from infection by following these guidelines.

- Wash your hands thoroughly before participating in class activities.
- Do not eat, drink, use tobacco products or chew gum during class.
- Clean the manikin properly before use.
  - For some manikins, this means vigorously wiping the manikin's face and the inside of its mouth with a clean gauze pad soaked with either a fresh solution of liquid chlorine bleach and water ($\frac{1}{4}$ cup sodium hypochlorite per gallon of tap water) or rubbing alcohol. The surfaces should remain wet for at least 1 minute before they are wiped dry with a second piece of clean, absorbent material.
  - For other manikins, it means changing the manikin's face. Your instructor will provide you with instructions for cleaning the type of manikin used in your class.
- Follow the guidelines from your instructor when practicing skills such as clearing a blocked airway with your finger.

PHYSICAL STRESS AND INJURY

Successful course completion requires full participation in classroom and skill sessions, as well as successful performance in skill and knowledge evaluations. You will be participating in strenuous activities, such as performing CPR on the floor. If you have a medical condition or disability that will prevent you from taking part in the skills practice sessions, please let your instructor know so that accommodations can be made. If you are unable to participate fully in the course, you may "audit" the course and participate as much as you can or desire. To audit a course, you must let the instructor know before the training begins. You will *not* be eligible to receive a course completion certificate.

*A person with a hepatitis B infection will test positive for the HBsAg. Most persons infected with hepatitis B will get better within a period of time. However, in some people hepatitis B infections will become chronic and will linger for much longer. These persons will continue to test positive for HBsAg. Their decision to participate in CPR training should be guided by their physician. After a person has had an acute hepatitis B infection, he or she will no longer test positive for the surface antigen but will test positive for the hepatitis B antibody (anti-HBs). Persons who have been vaccinated for hepatitis B will also test positive for the hepatitis antibody. A positive test for anti-HBs should not be confused with a positive test for HBsAG.

BEFORE GIVING CARE

RECOGNIZING AND RESPONDING TO AN EMERGENCY

Emergencies are often signaled by something unusual that catches your attention, such as—

- Unusual sights.
- Unusual appearances or behaviors.
- Unusual odors.
- Unusual noises.

It may be hard to recognize an emergency or sudden illness in some cases. The signals are not always easy to see or identify.

- If you think something is wrong, check the person. Ask questions. Questions may help you find out what is wrong.
- A person may deny anything is seriously wrong.

OVERCOMING BARRIERS TO ACT

Sometimes, even though people recognize that an emergency has occurred, they fail to act. The most common factors that keep people from responding are—

- The presence of other people.
- Being unsure of the ill or injured person's condition.
- The type of injury or illness.
- Fear of catching a disease.
- Fear of doing something wrong.
- Fear of being sued.
- Being unsure of when to call 9-1-1.

Ways to Overcome Barriers to Act

- Getting trained in first aid, cardiopulmonary resuscitation (CPR) or how to use an automated external defibrillator (AED).
  - Training to develop the confidence to act, which enables you to take charge until more advanced help arrives.
- Avoiding contact with blood or body fluids by using protective barriers and following standard precautions.

- Being familiar with Good Samaritan laws and obtaining consent.

GOOD SAMARITAN LAWS AND OBTAINING CONSENT

Good Samaritan Laws

All 50 states have enacted Good Samaritan laws that give legal protection to people who willingly give emergency care to an ill or injured person without accepting anything in return. These laws, which differ from state to state, usually protect citizens who act the same way that a "reasonable and prudent person" would if that person were in the same situation.

Developed to encourage people to help, these laws require the "Good Samaritan" to—

- Act in good faith.
- Not be deliberately negligent or reckless.
- Act within the scope of his or her training.
- Not abandon the person after starting to give care.

You should contact a legal professional or check at the local library to find out more about your state's Good Samaritan laws.

Obtaining Consent

Before giving first aid to a conscious adult, you must obtain his or her permission to give care. This permission is referred to as consent. A conscious person has the right to either refuse or accept care.

To obtain consent—

1. State your name.
2. Tell the person you are trained in first aid.
3. Ask the person if you can help.
4. Explain what you think may be wrong.
5. Explain what you plan to do.

Important points to remember include—

- **DO NOT** give care to a conscious person who refuses it.
- If a person does not give consent, you should still call 9-1-1 or the local emergency number.
- If the conscious person is an infant or child, get permission to give care from the parent or guardian if present.

- If the person is unconscious or unable to respond due to the illness or injury, consent is implied. Implied consent means you can assume that if the person could respond, he or she would agree to be cared for.
- Consent is also implied for an infant or child if a parent or guardian is not present or immediately available.

PREVENTING DISEASE TRANSMISSION

The risk of getting a disease while giving first aid is extremely low. When you follow standard precautions, you can reduce that risk even further. Always give care in ways that protect you and the person from disease transmission.

Whenever possible, you should—
- Avoid contact with blood and other body fluids.
- Avoid touching objects that may be soiled with blood or other body fluids.
- Cover any cuts, scrapes or sores prior to putting on protective equipment, such as gloves.
- Remove jewelry such as rings and watches before giving care.
- Avoid eating; drinking; smoking; applying cosmetics or lip balm; handling contact lenses; or touching your mouth, nose or eyes when you may be exposed to infectious materials or giving first aid.
- Place barriers between you and a person's blood or other body fluids using such items as—
  ○ Protective eyewear (Fig. 1-1).
  ○ CPR breathing barriers (e.g., resuscitation masks or face shields) (Fig. 1-2).

  ○ Disposable gloves (nitrile or vinyl)
  - Gloves soiled with blood are considered contaminated and a "biohazard," and should be disposed of properly (Fig. 1-3).

Be prepared by always having a properly equipped first aid kit nearby. (See Appendix A, Anatomy of a First Aid Kit, for a detailed list of required items.)

Cleaning Up a Blood Spill

If a blood spill occurs—
- Clean up the spill immediately or as soon as possible after the spill occurs.
- Use disposable gloves and other personal protective equipment when cleaning spills.
- Wipe up the spill with paper towels or other absorbent material.
- After the area has been wiped up, flood the area with a solution of $1\frac{1}{2}$ cup of liquid chlorine bleach to 1 gallon of fresh water (1 part bleach per 10 parts water) and allow it to stand for at least 10 minutes.
- Dispose of the contaminated material used to clean up the spill in a labeled biohazard container (Fig. 1-4).

OSHA Standards

Universal precautions are the federal Occupational Safety and Health Administration's (OSHA) required practices of infection control to protect employees from exposure to blood and other potentially infectious materials. These precautions require that all human blood and certain body substances be treated as if known to be infectious for hepatitis B virus, hepatitis C virus, human immunodeficiency virus (HIV) (the virus that causes acquired immunodeficiency syndrome [AIDS]) or other bloodborne pathogens. Other approaches to infection control are called standard precautions and Body Substance Isolation (BSI) precautions. These precautions mean that you should consider all body fluids and substances as infectious.

To get a copy of the OSHA Bloodborne Pathogens Standard (CFR 1910.1030) or for more information on the standard, refer to OSHA's Web site at **www.osha.gov.**

To learn more about reducing your risk of disease transmission, consider enrolling in the American Red Cross Bloodborne Pathogens Training: Preventing Disease Transmission course.

EMERGENCY ACTION STEPS

In any emergency, always follow three emergency action steps. Following these steps can minimize the confusion at an emergency scene.

1. **CHECK** the scene for safety; **CHECK** the ill or injured person.
   - **CHECK** the scene:
     - Is it safe?
     - What happened?
     - How many people are involved?
     - Is there immediate danger involved?
     - Is anyone else available to help?
   - **CHECK** for life-threatening conditions, such as—
     - Unconsciousness.
     - No breathing or trouble breathing.
     - No signs of life (breathing or movement).
     - Severe bleeding.

2. **CALL** 9-1-1 or the local emergency number when appropriate. Calling for help is often the most important action you can take to help an ill or injured person who needs care. It will start emergency medical care on its way as fast as possible.

3. **CARE** for the ill or injured person.
   If you are ALONE—
   - **Call First** (call 9-1-1 or the local emergency number) before giving care for—
     - An unconscious adult or adolescent age 12 years or older.
     - A witnessed sudden collapse of a child or infant.
     - An unconscious infant or child known to be at a high risk for heart problems.
   - **Care First** (give 2 minutes of care), then call 9-1-1 or the local emergency number for—
     - An unwitnessed collapse of an unconscious person younger than 12 years old.
     - Any victim of a drowning.

Call First situations are likely to be cardiac emergencies, such as sudden cardiac arrest or a witnessed sudden collapse of a child, in which time is critical. Research shows the shorter the time from when a person collapses to when CPR is initiated and when he or she is given the first shock with an automated external defibrillator (AED), the greater the chance of survival for an adult or child 1 year old or older. In **Care First** situations, the conditions are often related to breathing emergencies.

When to Call 9-1-1—Adult

Directions: Place a checkmark in the box next to any life-threatening conditions in which 9-1-1 or the local emergency number should be called.

- ☐ Minor bruise on the arm
- ☐ Unconsciousness
- ☐ Trouble breathing or breathing in a strange way
- ☐ Abrasion on the elbow
- ☐ Not breathing
- ☐ Cut lip
- ☐ No signs of life
- ☐ Persistent chest pain
- ☐ Severe bleeding that does not stop
- ☐ Mild sunburn on the shoulders
- ☐ Cramp in the thigh
- ☐ Deep burn to the face and neck
- ☐ Pressure or pain in the abdomen that does not go away
- ☐ Vomiting blood or passing blood
- ☐ Multiple seizures or seizures that last longer than 5 minutes
- ☐ Possible head, neck or back injuries
- ☐ Apparent poisoning
- ☐ Splinter in the finger
- ☐ Broken arm with bone showing through the skin
- ☐ Sudden severe headache or slurred speech
- ☐ Bloody nose

Note: The conditions listed above are not a complete list of life-threatening conditions and there are always exceptions. If you are confused or unsure about what to do, call 9-1-1 or the local emergency number.

When to Call 9-1-1—Child and Infant

Directions: Place a checkmark in the box next to any life-threatening conditions in which 9-1-1 or the local emergency number should be called.

- ☐ Minor bruise on the arm
- ☐ Sudden silence
- ☐ A cat scratch on the cheek
- ☐ Child found at the bottom of a pool with no signs of life
- ☐ Not breathing
- ☐ Bleeding from the knee that cannot be controlled
- ☐ Deep burn on the face

Note: The conditions listed above are not a complete list of life-threatening conditions and there are always exceptions. If you are confused or unsure about what to do, call 9-1-1 or the local emergency number.

Also, call 9-1-1 or the local emergency number if any of the following conditions exist:

- Fire or explosion
- The presence of poisonous gas
- Downed electrical wires
- Swiftly moving or rapidly rising water
- Motor vehicle collisions
- Persons who cannot be moved easily

CALLING 9-1-1 OR THE LOCAL EMERGENCY NUMBER

Instructions for Emergency Telephone Calls

EMERGENCY TELEPHONE NUMBERS
(Dial _____ for outside line)

EMS: _____

Fire: _____

Police: _____

_____

Poison Control Center: 800-222-1222 _____

Number of this telephone: _____

OTHER IMPORTANT TELEPHONE NUMBERS

Facility manager: _____

Facility maintenance: _____

Power company: _____

Gas company: _____

Weather bureau: _____

Name and address of medical facility with
24-hour emergency cardiac care:

_____

_____

INFORMATION FOR EMERGENCY CALL
Be prepared to give this information to the emergency medical services (EMS) dispatcher.

1. Location: _____
   - Street address: _____
   - City or town: _____
   - Directions (cross streets, roads, land-marks, etc.): _____
   - Exits and evacuation routes: _____
   _____

2. Telephone number from which the call is being made: _____

3. Caller's name: _____

4. What happened? _____

5. How many people are injured? _____

6. Condition of injured person(s): _____

7. Help (care) being given: _____

Note:
- *Do not hang up first. Let the EMS dispatcher hang up first.*
- *In cities with Enhanced 9-1-1 (E 9-1-1) systems, it is still important to know the information above for communication to the dispatcher. In many buildings, the telephone system may connect through a switchboard that will show only the corporate address rather than the specific facility from which you are calling. With mobile telephones, E 9-1-1 is not functional because there is no fixed location to identify on the dispatcher's screen, so sharing this information is the only way to provide it.*
- *This sample form can be posted by the telephone.*

9-1-1 and E 9-1-1 Systems

There are two types of 9-1-1 systems—Basic and Enhanced. A Basic 9-1-1 system automatically routes the emergency call to the Public Service Answering Point (PSAP) that handles the area where the phone is located. An Enhanced 9-1-1 system automatically displays the telephone number, address and name in which the phone is listed. If the caller is unable to remain on the line or is unable to speak or if the call is disconnected, the dispatcher can still obtain enough information to send help. Some 9-1-1 systems can reconnect a caller and transfer callers to other agencies or telephone numbers with a single button.

Information Line

Many 9-1-1 calls in the United States are not emergencies. For this reason, some cities have started using 3-1-1 (or similar) as a number for people to call for non-emergency situations. Find out if your area uses this number. Remember, your local emergency number is for just that— emergencies! So please use good judgment.

Wireless 9-1-1: Hundreds of Millions Served

Mobile phones are not associated with one fixed location or address, which can make it difficult to accurately determine the location of the caller or the emergency. Current and future development of the 9-1-1 system includes initiatives to integrate wireless technology more effectively. The Federal Communications Commission has adopted a variety of 9-1-1 rules aimed at improving the system's ability to locate mobile 9-1-1 callers. These rules apply to all mobile phones licensees, broadband personal communication services and certain special mobile radio licensees.

Because mobile 9-1-1 location information is not available everywhere, it is important to remember the following tips when using a mobile phone to call 9-1-1.

- Tell the call taker the location of the emergency right away.
- Give the call taker your wireless phone number so that if the call gets disconnected, he or she can call you back.
- If your wireless phone is not "initialized" (i.e., you do not have a contract for service with a wireless service provider) and your emergency call gets disconnected, you must call the emergency operator back because he or she does not have your telephone number and cannot contact you.
- Learn to use the designated number in your state for highway accidents or other non-life-threatening incidents. States often reserve specific numbers for these types of incidents. For example, "#77" is the number used for highway accidents in Virginia. The number to call for nonlife-threatening incidents in your state can be located in the front of your phone book.
- Do not program your phone to automatically dial 9-1-1 when one button such as the "9" key is pressed. Unintentional wireless 9-1-1 calls, which often occur when autodial keys are inadvertently pressed, cause problems for emergency service call centers.
- If your wireless phone came preprogrammed with the auto-dial 9-1-1 feature already turned on, turn this feature off. Check your user manual to find out how.
- Lock your keypad when you are not using your wireless phone. This action also prevents accidental calls to 9-1-1.

Sources:
DISPATCH Monthly Magazine, **www.911dispatch.com**. Accessed 6/24/04.

Federal Communications Commission, **www.fcc.gov/911/enhanced**. Accessed 6/24/04.

National Emergency Number Association, **www.nena.org**. Accessed 6/24/04.

REACHING AND MOVING AN ILL OR INJURED PERSON

"Do No Further Harm"

One of the most dangerous threats to a seriously injured person is unnecessary movement. Usually when giving care, you will not face dangers that require you to move a person. In most cases, you can follow the emergency steps (**CHECK—CALL—CARE**) where you find the person. Calling for help is the most important step you can take in an emergency to help the person in need of care.

Moving a seriously injured person can cause additional injury and pain and complicate the person's recovery. Therefore, you should move a person *only* under the following three situations:

1. When you are faced with immediate danger
2. When you have to get to another person who may have a more serious injury or illness
3. When you need to provide proper care

Once you decide that you must move a person based on the guidance above, you must quickly decide *how* to move the person. Carefully consider your safety and the safety of the person. Base your decision on the dangers you are facing, the size and condition of the person, your ability and condition and whether you have any help.

To avoid injuring yourself or the person, use your legs, not your back, when you bend. Bend at the knees and hips and avoid twisting your body. Walk forward when possible, taking small steps and looking where you are going.

Avoid twisting or bending anyone with a possible head, neck or back injury. Do not move a person who is too large to move comfortably.

Emergency Moves

WALKING ASSIST

To help a person who needs assistance walking to safety—

- Place the person's arm across your shoulders and hold it in place with one hand (Fig. 1-5A).
- Support the person with your other hand around the person's waist.
- Move the person to safety.
- A second responder, if present, can support the person in the same way on the other side (Fig. 1-5B).

PACK-STRAP CARRY

To move either a conscious or unconscious person—

- Position yourself with your back to the person.
- Cross the person's arms in front of you and grasp the person's wrists.
- Lean forward slightly and pull the person onto your back (Fig. 1-6).

TWO-PERSON SEAT CARRY

To carry a person who cannot walk and has no suspected head, neck or back injury—

- Put one arm under the person's thighs and the other across the person's back.
- Interlock your arms with those of a second responder under the person's legs and across the person's back (Fig. 1-7A).
- Lift the person in the "seat" formed by the responders' arms (Fig. 1-7B).
- Move the person to safety.

CLOTHES DRAG

To move a person who may have a head, neck or back injury—

- Gather the clothing behind the person's neck (Fig. 1-8).
- Pull the person to safety.
- While moving the person, cradle the head with the person's clothes and your hands.

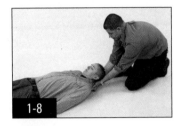
1-8

BLANKET DRAG

To move a person in an emergency situation when equipment is limited—

- Keep the person between you and the blanket.
- Gather half the blanket and place it against the person's side.
- Roll the person as a unit toward you.
- Reach over and place the blanket so that it will be positioned under the person.
- Roll the person onto the blanket.
- Gather the blanket at the head and move the person (Fig. 1-9).

1-9

FOOT DRAG

To move a person too large to carry or move otherwise—

- Firmly grasp the person's ankles and move backward.
- Pull the person in a straight line and be careful not to bump the person's head (Fig. 1-10).

1-10

Confined Spaces

A confined space is a space that is large enough and configured so that an employee can enter and perform assigned work. It has limited or restricted means of entry or exit (e.g., tanks, vessels, silos, storage bins, hoppers, vaults and pits are spaces that may have limited means of entry). They are not designed for continuous employee occupancy.

SKILL SHEET: WASHING HANDS

Wash your hands with soap and running water immediately after giving care even if you wore disposable gloves. It is important that you wash your hands correctly—

1. Turn on warm water.

2. Wet hands with water.
3. Apply liquid soap to hands.

4. Rub your hands together vigorously for at least 15 seconds, covering all surfaces of the hands and fingers.

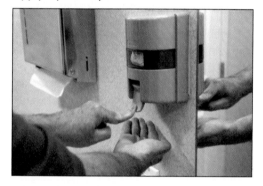

- Use soap and warm running water.
- Scrub nails by rubbing them against the palms of your hands.

5. Rinse your hands with water.
6. Dry your hands thoroughly with a paper towel.
7. Turn off the faucet using the paper towel.

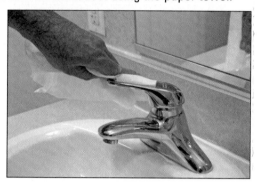

If hand-washing facilities are not readily available, use alcohol-based hand sanitizers or lotions to clean your hands, but not in place of hand washing with soap and water.

SKILL SHEET: REMOVING DISPOSABLE GLOVES

STEP 1: Partially remove the first glove.
- Pinch the glove at the wrist, being careful to touch only the glove's outside surface.

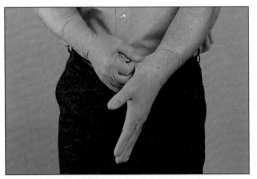

- Pull the glove toward the fingertips without completely removing it. The glove is now partly inside out.

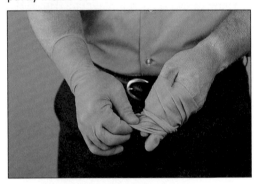

STEP 2: Remove the second glove.
- With your partially gloved hand, pinch the outside surface of the second glove.
- Pull the second glove toward the fingertips until it is inside out, and then remove it completely.

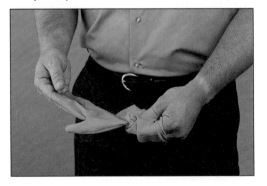

STEP 3: Finish removing both gloves.
- Grasp both gloves with your free hand.
- Touch only the clean interior surface of the glove.

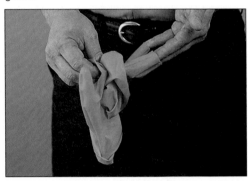

STEP 4: After removing both gloves—
- Discard gloves in an appropriate container.
- Wash your hands thoroughly.

CHECKING AN ILL OR INJURED PERSON

CHECKING A CONSCIOUS PERSON

For the purpose of first aid, an adult is defined as someone about 12 years of age or older. Someone between the ages of about 1 and 12 years old is considered a child. When using pediatric AED equipment, a child is someone between the ages of 1 and 8 or weighing less than 55 pounds. An infant is someone less than about 1 year of age.

First, check the scene. Then, check the person for life-threatening conditions. Tell the person not to move and get consent to give care. If there are any life-threatening conditions, call 9-1-1 or the local emergency number.

If there are no life-threatening conditions and the person is conscious, ask the person—
- What is your name?
- What happened?
- Where do you feel any pain or discomfort?
- Do you feel numbness or loss of sensation? If so, where?
- Do you have any allergies? If so, what?
- Do you have any medical conditions or are you taking any medications? If so, what conditions do you have or what medications are you taking?
- When did you last eat or drink anything?

Give this information to emergency medical services (EMS) personnel when they arrive.

Checking an Adult from Head to Toe
- Tell the person not to move any body part that hurts.
- Begin the check at the top of the head, face, ears, nose and mouth.
- Look for cuts, bruises, bumps, depressions, bleeding or fluid.
- Feel the person's forehead with the back of your (bare) hand for temperature (and moisture).
- Look at the coloring of the person's face and lips.
- Notice how the skin looks and feels. Note if it is red, pale or ashen.
- Look over the body, starting at the head, scanning down the torso, arms and hands then legs and feet.

- Watch the person for signals of pain and listen for sounds of pain.
- Watch for changes in consciousness and breathing.
- When the check is complete, have the person rest comfortably while you care for the conditions you find.

Checking a Child or Infant from Toe to Head
- When checking a child for nonlife-threatening conditions, observe the child before touching him or her.
- Look for signals that indicate changes in consciousness, any trouble breathing and any apparent injuries or conditions.
- Get at eye level with the child (Fig. 2-1).
- Talk slowly and in a friendly manner.
- Use simple words.
- Ask questions that the child can answer easily.
- When you begin your check, begin at the toes instead of the head. Checking in this order gives the child a chance to get used to the process and allows him or her to see what is going on.

2-1

Giving Care
Once you complete the examination, give care for any specific injuries you find. To give care for the person until EMS personnel arrive, follow these general guidelines:
- Do no further harm.
- Monitor the "**ABC**s"—Airway, Breathing and Circulation.
- Help the person rest in the most comfortable position.
- Keep the person from getting chilled or over-heated.
- Reassure the person.
- Give any specific care needed.

Prioritizing Care Activity—Adult

In an emergency with more than one victim, you may need to determine who needs help first. This is called prioritizing care.

Directions: Read the following emergency situations. Circle the victim in each emergency situation who has a life-threatening condition and needs help **first.**

Emergency Situation 1   You are returning to work from a lunch break when you hear the sound of screeching wheels and then a crash. There has been a vehicle accident between a car that was leaving the parking lot and a truck. After checking the scene, you approach to check the victims. Which person needs help first?

Victim 1   The driver of the truck who gets out to examine the driver and passenger of the car.

Victim 2   The driver of the car who is moaning in pain and appears to have a cut on his face.

Victim 3   The passenger of the car who is not moving at all and appears to be unconscious.

Emergency Situation 2   You are at a construction site when you hear a loud, crashing noise and then some screaming. Parts of a structure and some scaffolding have collapsed, injuring several people. Which victim needs help first?

Victim 1   The person who gets up slowly and stumbles away from the debris.

Victim 2   The person who is bleeding severely and appears to have a broken arm.

Victim 3   The person who is lying on the ground and tells you that her ankle hurts and she may have twisted it.

Emergency Situation 3   You and some co-workers have been working hard outside. It is a hot, humid day and all of you are exhausted. You take a short break and go to the cooler for some water. When you return, three of your co-workers are sitting down; they do not look well. One of them tries to stand up but falls over. Which person needs help first?

Victim 1   The person who fell over and is now sitting on the ground. His skin appears moist and ashen, and he is sweating profusely.

Victim 2   The person who has hot, red, dry skin. He appears to be unconscious and does not respond when you ask how he is feeling.

Victim 3   The person who is sweating heavily and whose skin appears pale and moist. He is complaining that he is tired.

Prioritizing Care Activity—Child

In an emergency with more than one victim, you may need to determine who needs help first. This is called prioritizing care.

Directions: Read the following emergency situations. Circle the victim in each emergency situation who has a life-threatening condition and needs help **first**.

Emergency Situation 1   You are the first person to stop on a busy highway to assist at an accident scene. Who needs help first?

Victim 1   The adult driver who is calling for help but who otherwise appears uninjured.

Victim 2   The child who is seated in a car seat in the back middle passenger seat and who is not moving and appears to be unconscious.

Victim 3   The older child who is seated behind the mother and crying. You see a small cut on his right lower leg.

Emergency Situation 2   Three children playing in a tree house in the backyard suddenly tumble to the ground when the tree house falls to one side. Who needs help first?

Victim 1   The child who has a gash on his forehead, which is bleeding.

Victim 2   The child who is crying and trying to remove her arm, which is trapped between boards, but who does not appear to be bleeding.

Victim 3   The child who was hit by falling boards who is lying quietly, appears unconscious and is bleeding from a gash on his arm.

Emergency Situation 3   You go to a cafeteria for lunch. You see a young mother feeding her children when you hear a crash. Who needs help first?

Victim 1   The crying toddler who fell from her high chair.

Victim 2   The school-aged child who looks panicked and is clutching his throat.

Victim 3   The mother who is bleeding from her hand.

Prioritizing Care Activity—Infant

In an emergency with more than one victim, you may need to determine who needs help first. This is called prioritizing care.

Directions: Read the following emergency situations. Circle the victim in each emergency situation who has a life-threatening condition and needs help **first.**

Emergency Situation 1   You are at a friend's home having coffee. Your friend is babysitting a 7-month-old infant. Your friend's children, a 4-year-old and a 6-year-old, are quietly playing with the infant in the living room. You suddenly hear a crash and the older children screaming. Dashing into the room, you find several victims. Who needs help first?

Victim 1   The 7-month-old infant who is unconscious on the floor. (There is a piggy bank near her and her face is lying on some coins that are scattered about.)

Victim 2   The 6-year-old who is lying on the floor screaming with a bookcase toppled over close to him. He is holding his arm and has a cut on his head.

Victim 3   The 4-year-old who is lying nearby with books, bookends and some decorative glass figures tumbled around him. He is bleeding from the head and crying.

Emergency Situation 2   At a family party, two infants are put to sleep on a bed. When you go to check on them you find that both have either rolled or crept off onto the floor. You have two victims. Who needs help first?

Victim 1   The infant who is crying and holding his arm at an unusual angle.

Victim 2   The infant who appears unconscious, but there is no blood or apparent deformity present.

Emergency Situation 3   On a busy street, a driver swerves to avoid a jaywalker and goes over the curb, coming to a stop on the sidewalk after hitting several people and knocking over two strollers, each with an infant strapped in. Who needs help first?

Victim 1   The man who was knocked down but is getting up again and who appears dazed but not seriously injured.

Victim 2   The younger infant who is slumped sideways in the stroller and appears unconscious.

Victim 3   The older infant who is crying and bleeding from a cut on his arm.

Victim 4   The 3-year-old child who is sitting on the pavement crying, but appears uninjured.

RECOGNIZING AND CARING FOR SHOCK

Shock is a life-threatening condition in which not enough blood is being delivered to all parts of the body and body systems, and organs begin to fail. A person showing signals of shock needs immediate medical attention. Shock is likely to develop after any serious injury or illness including severe bleeding, serious internal injury, significant fluid loss or other conditions. The goals of first aid are to get help quickly and give care to minimize shock while caring for the injury or illness.

Signals of Shock

The signals that indicate a person may be going into shock include—

- Restlessness or irritability.
- Altered level of consciousness.
- Nausea or vomiting.
- Rapid breathing and pulse.
- Pale or ashen, cool, moist skin.
- Excessive thirst.

Care for Shock

- Make sure that 9-1-1 or the local emergency number has been called.
- Continue to monitor the person's ABCs.
- Control any external bleeding.
- Keep the person from getting chilled or overheated.
- Elevate the legs about 12 inches if a head, neck or back injury or if broken bones in the hips or legs are not suspected (Fig. 2-2).
- Comfort and reassure the person until EMS personnel arrive and take over.

Do not give the person anything to eat or drink, even though he or she is likely to be thirsty. The person's condition may be severe enough to require surgery, in which case it is better if the stomach is empty.

2-2

CHECKING AN UNCONSCIOUS PERSON

If you find that the person is unconscious and 9-1-1 or the local emergency number has been called, find out if there are other conditions that threaten the person's life. Always check to see if an unconscious person—

- Has an open airway.
- Shows signs of life (movement or breathing).
- Is bleeding severely.

An easy way to remember this is to think **"ABC,"** which stands for:

- **A**irway—Open the airway.
- **B**reathing—Check for movement or breathing.
- **C**irculation—Check for signs of life (including a pulse for a child or infant) and severe bleeding.

Because children and infants are smaller than adults, you do not have to tilt their heads back quite as far to open their airway. Tilting the head back too far can also block the airway (Fig. 2-3A-C).

2-3A

2-3B

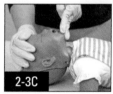
2-3C

Unlike adults, children seldom initially suffer a cardiac emergency. Instead, they suffer a breathing emergency that results in a cardiac emergency. For a child or infant, check for a pulse for no more than 10 seconds. For a child, you would need to feel for a carotid pulse (Fig. 2-4A) and for an infant, the brachial pulse (Fig. 2-4B).

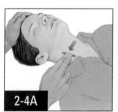
2-4A

2-4B

ROLLING A PERSON FACE-UP

If an unconscious person is face-down, you need to roll the person onto his or her back.
Position yourself so you are facing the back of the person's head. Move the arm that is closest to you up next to the head. Place your hands at the back of the neck and your other hand on the hip. Gently roll the person toward you, keeping the head, neck and back in a straight line (Fig. 2-5). Once the person is on his or her back, you need to open the airway.

2-5

SEVERE BLEEDING

Check for severe bleeding by quickly looking over the person's body from head to toe for signals such as blood-soaked clothing or blood spurting out of a wound. Bleeding usually looks worse than it is. A small amount of blood on a slick surface or mixed with water almost always looks like a great deal of blood. It is not always easy to recognize severe bleeding.

RECOVERY POSITION

If you are alone and have to leave the person for any reason, such as to call for help or get an AED, place the person in a recovery position. Placing a person in a recovery position will help the airway remain open and clear if he or she vomits.

To place a person in a recovery position, kneel at the person's side so you can support the body at the shoulder and at the hip. Take the arm farthest away from you and move it up next to the head. Take the other arm and cross it over the chest. Then, bend the leg closest to you. Supporting the shoulder and hip, gently roll the person away from you without twisting the body. Be careful to support the head so that it angles toward the ground. This will allow fluids to drain away from the throat.

If the person has been in the recovery position for 30 minutes or more and begins to show signals of loss of circulation to the lower arm (such as pale, ashen or grayish skin that is cool to the touch), turn him or her to the opposite side.

If you suspect a head, neck or back injury and a clear, open airway can be maintained, **do not** move the person unnecessarily. If a clear airway cannot be maintained or if you must leave the person to get help or get an AED, move the person to his or her side while keeping the head, neck or back in a straight line by placing him or her in a modified H.A.IN.E.S. (High Arm in Endangered Spine) recovery position (Fig. 2-6A-B).

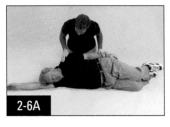
2-6A

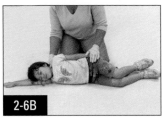
2-6B

SKILL SHEET: CHECKING AN ILL OR INJURED PERSON

For Adult (Age 12 or Older)

> **Tip:** Wear disposable gloves and personal protective equipment.

1. **CHECK** scene, then **CHECK** the person.
2. Tap shoulder and shout, "Are you okay?"
3. If no response, **CALL** 9-1-1.

> **Tip:** If an unconscious person is face-down—Roll face-up supporting the head, neck and back.

4. Open the airway (tilt head, lift chin). **CHECK** for movement and breathing for no more than 10 seconds.

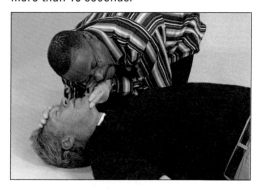

5. If not breathing, give **2** rescue breaths.

> **Tip:** Irregular, gasping or shallow breaths are **not** effective.

> **Tip:** Also quickly scan for severe bleeding.

> **Tip:** If checking an unconscious child or infant and breaths go in, **CHECK** for a pulse for no more than 10 seconds (see Fig. 2-4 A-B on p. 16).

6. If the person is breathing, place him or her in a recovery position and monitor **ABCs**.

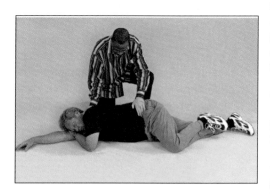

BREATHING EMERGENCIES AND CONSCIOUS CHOKING— ADULT, CHILD OR INFANT

BREATHING EMERGENCIES

A breathing emergency occurs when a person is having trouble breathing (respiratory distress) or cannot breathe at all (respiratory arrest). Breathing emergencies are life threatening (Fig. 3-1).

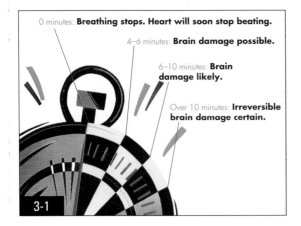

0 minutes: **Breathing stops. Heart will soon stop beating.**

4–6 minutes: **Brain damage possible.**

6–10 minutes: **Brain damage likely.**

Over 10 minutes: **Irreversible brain damage certain.**

3-1

Causes of Breathing Emergencies

- A partially obstructed airway
- Illness
- Chronic conditions, such as asthma
- Electrocution
- Heart attack
- Injury to the head, chest, lungs or abdomen
- Allergic reaction
- Drugs
- Poisoning
- Emotional distress

Signals of Breathing Emergencies— Adult

- The person has trouble breathing (Fig. 3-2).
  - Breathing is slow or rapid.
  - Breaths are unusually deep or shallow.
- The person is gasping for breath.
- The person is wheezing, gurgling or making high-pitched noises.

3-2

- In an unconscious adult, you may detect irregular, gasping or shallow breaths. These are known as agonal breaths. **DO NOT** confuse this with normal breathing.
- The person's skin is unusually moist or cool and has a flushed, pale, ashen or bluish appearance.
- The person feels—
  - Short of breath.
  - Dizzy or light-headed.
  - Pain in the chest or tingling in the hands, feet or lips.
  - Apprehensive or fearful.

Signals of Breathing Emergencies— Child and Infant

- Agitation
- Unusually fast or slow breathing
- Drowsiness
- Noisy breathing
- Pale, ashen, flushed or bluish skin color
- Breathing trouble increases
- Change in the level of consciousness
- Increased heart rate
- Sudden silence

It is very important to recognize breathing emergencies in children and infants and to act before the heart stops beating. Adults' hearts frequently stop beating because they are diseased. Infants' and children's hearts, however, are usually healthy. When an infant or child's heart stops, it is usually the result of a breathing emergency.

Some Conditions that Cause Breathing Emergencies

ASTHMA Asthma is a condition that narrows the air passages. An asthma attack happens when a trigger, such as exercise, cold air, allergens or other irritants, causes the airway to swell and narrow. This makes breathing difficult, which is frightening. You can often tell when a person is having an asthma attack by the hoarse whistling sound he or she makes while exhaling. This sound, known as wheezing, occurs because air becomes trapped in the lungs. Coughing after exercise, crying or laughing are other signals that an asthma attack is taking place. Usually, people diagnosed with asthma control their attacks with medications. These medications stop the muscle spasm and open the airway, which makes breathing easier. For more information on asthma see Appendix G.

EMPHYSEMA Emphysema is a disease that involves damage to the lungs' air sacs. It is a chronic (long-lasting or frequently reoccurring) disease that worsens over time. The most common signal of emphysema is shortness of breath. Exhaling is extremely difficult. In advanced cases, the affected person may feel restless, confused and weak, and may even go into respiratory or cardiac arrest.

BRONCHITIS Bronchitis is a condition that causes the bronchial tubes to become swollen and irritated. This inflammation causes a build-up of mucus that blocks the passage of air and air exchange in the lungs. A person with bronchitis will typically have a persistent cough and may feel tightness in the chest and have trouble breathing. As with emphysema, the person may also feel restless, confused and weak, and may even go into respiratory or cardiac arrest.

HYPERVENTILATION Hyperventilation occurs when a person breathes faster and more shallowly than normal. When this happens, the body does not take in enough oxygen to meet its demands. People who are hyperventilating feel as if they cannot get enough air. Often they are afraid and anxious or seem confused. They may say that they feel dizzy or that their fingers and toes feel numb and tingly.

ALLERGIC REACTION Allergic reactions also can cause breathing problems. At first, the reaction may appear to be just a rash and a feeling of tightness in the chest and throat, but this condition can become life threatening. The person's face, neck and tongue may swell, closing the airway. A severe allergic reaction can cause a condition called anaphylactic shock, also known as anaphylaxis. During anaphylaxis, air passages may swell and restrict a person's breathing. Signals of anaphylaxis include rashes; tightness in the chest and throat; and swelling of the face, neck and tongue. The person may also feel dizzy or confused. Some people know that they are allergic to certain substances. They may have learned to avoid these things and may carry medication to reverse the allergic reaction. For more information on allergic reactions and treatment for anaphylaxis see Appendix H.

CONSCIOUS CHOKING

Adult or Child

- Choking is a breathing emergency.
- It is a common injury that can lead to death.
- If a person is conscious and cannot cough, speak or breathe, assume that the airway is blocked.
- A person who is choking may clutch at his or her throat (Fig. 3-3). This gesture is the universal sign of choking.
- Common causes of choking include—
  - Trying to swallow large pieces of poorly chewed food.
  - Eating while talking excitedly or laughing, or eating too fast.
  - Walking, playing or running with food or objects in the mouth.

  Additional causes of adult choking are drinking alcohol before or during meals (alcohol dulls

3-3

the nerves that aid swallowing) and wearing dentures (dentures make it difficult to sense whether food is fully chewed before it is swallowed).

A person with a partially blocked airway can still move air to and from the lungs, so he or she can cough to try to dislodge the object. A person with a completely blocked airway cannot cough, speak or breathe. This person needs back blows and abdominal thrusts to clear the airway. Give chest thrusts instead of abdominal thrusts to a choking person who is obviously pregnant or known to be pregnant or too big for you to reach around (Fig. 3-4A). If you are alone and choking, lean over and press your abdomen against any firm object (Fig. 3-4B). You can give yourself abdominal thrusts by using your hands (Fig. 3-4C). Give a choking victim in a wheelchair abdominal thrusts (Fig. 3-4D).

3-4A

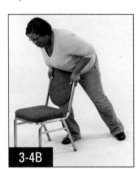

3-4B

3-4C

3-4D

Infant

Choking is a major cause of injury and death in infants. An infant can easily swallow small objects or small pieces of food, which can then block the airway. Additional reasons for choking include—

- The infant's airway has not fully developed.
- The infant has not fully developed his or her eating skills.

An infant with a partial airway obstruction can still move air to and from the lungs, so he or she can cough in an attempt to dislodge the

object. An infant with a complete airway obstruction is unable to cough, cry or breathe.

To free the blockage in the infant's airway, you can give back blows and chest thrusts, either standing or sitting, as long as the infant is supported on your thigh and the head is lower than the chest. If the infant is large or your hands are too small to adequately support the infant, you may prefer to sit.

CHOKING PREVENTION FOR CHILDREN AND INFANTS

Dangerous Foods

Do not feed any round, firm food to children younger than 4 years of age unless the food is chopped completely. The following foods can be choking hazards:

- Hot dogs
- Nuts
- Chunks of meat or cheese
- Hard or sticky candy
- Popcorn
- Raw carrots
- Whole grapes
- Chunks of peanut butter

Dangerous Household Items

Keep the following household items stored safely out of reach of infants and children:

- Balloons
- Coins
- Marbles
- Small toy parts
- Pen or marker caps
- Small, button-type batteries
- Small, compressible toys that can fit entirely into a child's mouth
- Plastic bags

Action Steps to Prevent Choking

- Seat children in a high chair or at a table while they eat.
- Do not let children eat too fast.
- Give infants soft food that they do not need to chew.
- Supervise children while they eat.
- Cut food into small bites for infants and young children, and teach them to chew their food well.

RESCUE BREATHING— CHILD OR INFANT

It is important to remember the following about rescue breathing:

- Injury or illness can sometimes cause a child or infant to stop breathing.
- Rescue breathing is the process of breathing air into a person who is not breathing.
- The vital organs depend on a constant supply of oxygen to function properly.
- It is natural to feel uncomfortable about making mouth-to-mouth contact with a stranger, even though the risk of disease transmission is very low.
- A resuscitation mask or face-shield [also known as a cardiopulmonary resuscitation (CPR) breathing barrier], may reduce the risk of disease transmission between the responder and the person.
- Rescue breathing should not be delayed because you do not have a breathing barrier or know how to use one.

SPECIAL SITUATIONS

Air in the Stomach

When you are giving rescue breaths, be careful to avoid forcing air into the person's stomach instead of the lungs. This may happen if you breathe too long, breathe too hard or do not open the airway far enough. Air in the stomach can cause the person to vomit and suffer complications, and it also makes it harder for the diaphragm, the large muscle that controls breathing, to move. This makes it harder for the lungs to fill with air.

Vomiting

If the person begins to vomit, remove the breathing barrier, then—

1. Turn the person's head and body together as a unit to the side (Fig. 4-1).
2. Wipe out the person's mouth with your finger.

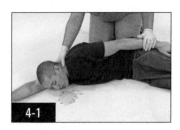

4-1

3. Carefully reposition the person on his or her back.
4. Replace the breathing barrier.
5. Open the airway.
6. Continue with rescue breathing as needed.

Mouth-to-Nose Breathing

If you are unable to make a tight enough seal over the person's mouth, you can breathe into the nose.

1. With the head tilted back, close the mouth by pushing on the chin.
2. Seal your mouth around the person's nose and breathe into the nose (Fig. 4-2).
3. If possible, open the person's mouth between rescue breaths to let the air out.

4-2

Mouth-to-Stoma Breathing

A stoma is an opening in the front of the neck through which a person whose larynx has been removed or partially removed breathes (Fig. 4-3A).

To care for a person with a stoma—

1. Look, listen and feel for breathing with your ear over the stoma (Fig. 4-3B).
2. Give breaths into the stoma, breathing at the same rate as for mouth-to-mouth breathing (Fig. 4-3C).

4-3A

4-3B

4-3C

3. When giving mouth-to-stoma breathing, air may leak through the nose and mouth, diminishing the amount of rescue breaths that reach the lungs. If this occurs, you need to seal the nose and mouth with your hand to prevent air from escaping during rescue breathing.

4. Remove your mouth from the stoma between breaths to let the air flow back out.

Drowning

To care for a person who is unconscious and not breathing—

1. Attempt rescue breaths.
2. If air does not go in, reposition the airway and give breaths again.
3. If breaths do not go in, give care for unconscious choking.
4. Once the airway is clear, give rescue breathing or CPR as needed.

Head, Neck or Back Injuries

To care for a person who you suspect has a head, neck or back injury—

- Try to minimize movement of the head and neck when opening the airway.
- Tilt the head and lift the chin to open the airway.

CARDIAC EMERGENCIES

PREVENTING HEART DISEASE

Guidelines for a Heart-Healthy Lifestyle

- Eat a balanced diet that limits the intake of saturated fat and cholesterol.
- Participate in continuous, vigorous physical activity for 20 to 30 minutes or more at least three times a week.
- Have blood pressure and cholesterol levels checked regularly.
- Maintain appropriate weight.
- Avoid tobacco use. Do not start smoking and if you do smoke, quit.

Heart-Healthy I.Q.

The following statements represent a heart-healthy lifestyle that can reduce your chances of heart disease. Check each statement that reflects your lifestyle.

- ☐ I do not smoke and I avoid inhaling the smoke of others.
- ☐ I eat a balanced diet that limits my intake of saturated fat and cholesterol.
- ☐ I participate in continuous, vigorous physical activity for 20 to 30 minutes or more at least three times a week.
- ☐ I have my blood pressure checked regularly.
- ☐ I maintain an appropriate weight.

If you did not check two or more of the statements, you should consider making changes in your lifestyle now.

RECOGNIZING A HEART ATTACK

Signals of a Heart Attack

- Persistent chest pain or pressure (a primary signal of a heart attack) that lasts longer than 3 to 5 minutes or goes away and comes back
- Chest pain spreading to the shoulders, neck, jaw, stomach or arms (Fig. 5-1)
- Shortness of breath or trouble breathing
- Nausea or vomiting
- Dizziness, light-headedness or fainting

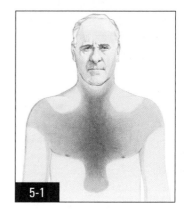

5-1

- Pale, ashen (grayish) or bluish skin
- Sweating
- Denial of signals

Both men and women experience the most common heart attack signal, which is chest pain or discomfort. But women are somewhat more likely than men to experience some of the other warning signals, particularly shortness of breath, nausea/vomiting and back or jaw pain. Women also tend to delay telling others about their signals to avoid bothering or worrying others.

CARE FOR A HEART ATTACK

- Call 9-1-1 or the local emergency number.
- Have the person stop what he or she is doing and rest comfortably.
- Loosen any tight or uncomfortable clothing.
- Closely watch the person until emergency medical services (EMS) personnel arrive. Notice any changes in the person's appearance or behavior.
- Try to obtain information about the person's condition.
- Comfort the person.
- Assist with medication, if prescribed.
- Offer an aspirin if medically appropriate and local protocols allow.
- Be prepared to give cardiopulmonary resuscitation (CPR) if the person's heart stops beating and use an automated external defibrillator (AED) if one is available and you are trained to do so.

ASPIRIN CAN LESSEN HEART ATTACK DAMAGE

You may be able to help a conscious person who is showing early signals of a heart attack by offering him or her an appropriate dose of aspirin when the signals first begin. However, you should *never* delay calling 9-1-1 to do this. *Always* call 9-1-1 as soon as you recognize the signals, and then help the person to be comfortable before you give the aspirin.

Then, if the person is able to take medicine by mouth, ask if he or she—

- Is allergic to aspirin.
- Has a stomach ulcer or stomach disease.
- Is taking any blood thinners, such as Warfarin™ or Coumadin™.
- Has been told by a doctor to not take aspirin.

If the person answers no to all of these questions, you may offer him or her two chewable (162 mg) baby aspirins, or up to one 5-grain (325 mg) adult aspirin tablet with a small amount of water. Be sure that you only give aspirin and not acetaminophen (Tylenol) or ibuprofen (Motrin or Advil), which are painkillers. Likewise, do not use coated aspirin products or products meant for multiple uses such as cold, fever and headache.

You may also offer these doses of aspirin if you have cared for the person and he or she has regained consciousness and is able to take the aspirin by mouth.

CARDIAC CHAIN OF SURVIVAL

Cardiac arrest is the condition in which the heart stops functioning altogether. CPR alone is not enough to help someone survive cardiac arrest. Emergency medical care is needed as soon as possible. This is why it is so important to call

5-2

9-1-1 or the local emergency number immediately. Although rare, children and teenagers can experience cardiac arrest.

The greatest chance of survival from cardiac arrest occurs when the following sequence of events happens as rapidly as possible (Fig. 5-2):

1. **Early recognition and early access.** The sooner 9-1-1 or the local emergency number is called, the sooner early advanced medical care arrives.
2. **Early CPR.** Early CPR helps circulate blood that contains oxygen to the vital organs until an AED is ready to use or advanced medical personnel arrive.
3. **Early defibrillation.** Most persons with sudden cardiac arrest need an electric shock called defibrillation. Each minute that defibrillation is delayed reduces the chance of survival by about 10 percent.
4. **Early advanced medical care.** This is given by trained medical personnel who give further care and transport to hospital facilities.

In the Cardiac Chain of Survival, each link of the chain depends on and is connected to the other links. It is very important to recognize and start CPR promptly and continue it until an AED is available or EMS personnel arrive and take over. Any delay in calling 9-1-1 or the local emergency number, starting CPR and using an AED makes it less likely the person will survive. Remember, you, the lay responder, are the first link in the Cardiac Chain of Survival.

CPR AND UNCONSCIOUS CHOKING—ADULT, CHILD OR INFANT

CPR—ADULT

An adult in cardiac arrest is unconscious and shows no other signs of life (movement or breathing). Loss of these signs of life can indicate cardiac arrest. A combination of chest compressions and rescue breaths can help circulate blood containing oxygen to vital organs (cardiopulmonary resuscitation or CPR).

CPR—CHILD

Unlike adults, children seldom initially suffer a cardiac emergency. Instead, they suffer a breathing emergency that results in a cardiac emergency. Motor vehicle crashes, drowning, smoke inhalation, poisoning, airway obstruction, firearm injuries and falls all are common causes of breathing emergencies that can develop into a cardiac emergency. A cardiac emergency can also result from an acute respiratory condition, such as a severe asthma attack.

CPR—INFANT

A cardiac emergency in an otherwise healthy infant is uncommon unless it is preceded by trauma or a breathing emergency, like drowning or choking, and the infant has not been successfully resuscitated in time. Infants born with genetic or congenital problems also may be at increased risk for cardiac emergencies because of problems with the heart's structure or function.

CPR FOR CHILDREN AND INFANTS

The CPR technique you use on children and infants will be slightly different because infants and children have smaller bodies and faster breathing and heart rates. You will need to adjust your hand position and compression depth (Fig 6-1A-D).

Continue CPR until—
- Another trained person takes over CPR for you.
- Emergency medical services (EMS) personnel arrive and take over care of the person.
- An automated external defibrillator (AED) becomes readily available.
- You are exhausted and unable to continue.
- The scene becomes unsafe.
- Signs of life return.

TWO RESPONDERS AVAILABLE

If two responders trained in CPR are at the scene, you should both identify yourselves as being trained in CPR. One should call 9-1-1 or the local emergency number for help, if this has not been done, while the other provides CPR. If the first responder is tired and needs help—
- The first responder should tell the second responder to take over.
- The second responder should immediately begin CPR starting with chest compressions.

UNCONSCIOUS CHOKING

If you attempt rescue breaths but are unable to make the person's chest clearly rise, you must act quickly to get air into the person. The care for an unconscious choking person is very similar to the skill of CPR, with the exception that you look for (and remove) a foreign object between compressions and breaths. Chest compressions are used to help force air from the person's lungs to dislodge the object.

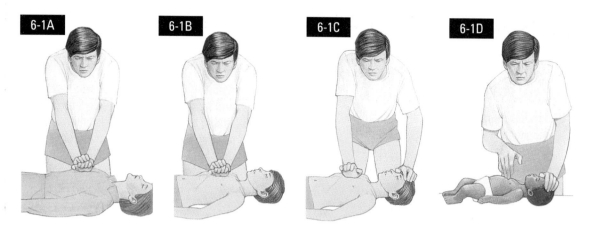

CPR SKILL COMPARISON CHART

Skill Components	Adult	Child	Infant
HAND POSITION:	Two hands in center of chest (on lower half of sternum)	One or two hands in center of chest (on lower half of sternum)	Two or three fingers on lower half of chest (one finger width below nipple line)
COMPRESS:	1½ to 2 inches	1 to 1½ inches	½ to 1 inch
BREATHE:	Until the chest rises (about 1 second per breath)	Until the chest rises (about 1 second per breath)	Until the chest rises (about 1 second per breath)
CYCLE:	30 compressions 2 breaths	30 compressions 2 breaths	30 compressions 2 breaths
RATE:	30 compressions in about 18 seconds (100 compressions per minute)	30 compressions in about 18 seconds (100 compressions per minute)	30 compressions in about 18 seconds (100 compressions per minute)

AED—ADULT

THE ROLE OF CPR

- Cardiopulmonary resuscitation (CPR) begun immediately and continued until defibrillation is available helps to circulate blood that contains oxygen to the brain and other vital organs.
- CPR is performed in conjunction with the use of an automated external defibrillator (AED).

USING AN AED ON AN ADULT (AGE 8 AND OLDER)

- An AED is a device that analyzes the heart's electrical rhythm and, if necessary, prompts you to deliver a shock to a person experiencing sudden cardiac arrest.
- Defibrillation is a process of delivering an electrical shock that disrupts a heart's electrical activity long enough to allow the heart to spontaneously develop an effective rhythm on its own.
- If the AED prompts you "No shock advised," you may have to perform CPR.

AED Precautions

- Do not touch the person while the AED is analyzing. Touching or moving the person may affect the analysis.
- Do not touch the person while the device is defibrillating. You could be shocked.
- Prior to shocking a person with an AED, be sure no one is touching or in contact with the person or the resuscitation equipment.
- Do not use alcohol to wipe the victim's chest dry. Alcohol is flammable.
- Do not defibrillate someone when around flammable materials, such as gasoline or free-flowing oxygen.
- Do not use an AED in a moving vehicle. Movement may affect the analysis.
- Do not use an AED on a person who is in contact with water. Move the person away from puddles of water or swimming pools or out of the rain before defibrillating.

- Do not use an AED and/or electrode pads designed for adults on a child age 8 and under or weighing less than 55 pounds unless pediatric pads specific to the device are not available; local protocols may differ on this and should be followed.
- Do not use an AED on a person wearing a nitroglycerin patch or other patch on the chest. With a gloved hand, remove any patches before attaching the device.
- Do not use a mobile phone or radio within 6 feet of the AED. This may interrupt analysis.

Special AED Situations

Some situations require you to pay special attention when using an AED. Be familiar with these situations and know how to respond appropriately. Always use common sense when using an AED and follow the manufacturer's recommendations.

WET ENVIRONMENTS If a person has been removed from water, dry the person's chest and attach the AED. The person should not be in a puddle of water, nor should the responder be kneeling in a puddle of water when operating an AED.

If it is raining, take steps to ensure that the person is as dry as possible and sheltered from the rain. Ensure that the person's chest is wiped dry. Minimize delaying defibrillation, though, when taking steps to provide for a dry environment. The electrical current of an AED is very directional between the electrode pads. AEDs are very safe, even in rain and snow, when all precautions and manufacturer's operating instructions are followed.

IMPLANTABLE DEVICES Some people whose hearts are weak and may beat too slow, skip beats or beat in a rhythm that is too fast may have had a pacemaker implanted. These small devices are sometimes located in the area below the right collarbone. There may be a small lump that can be felt under the skin. Sometimes the pacemaker is placed somewhere else. Other individuals may have an implantable cardioverter-defibrillator (ICD), a miniature

7-1

version of an AED, which acts to automatically recognize and restore abnormal heart rhythms (Fig. 7-1). Sometimes, a person's heart beats irregularly, even if the person has a pacemaker or ICD.

If the implanted device is visible or you know that the person has one, do not place the defibrillation pads directly over the device. This may interfere with the delivery of the shock. Adjust pad placement if necessary and continue to follow the established protocol. If you are not sure, use the AED if needed. It will not harm the person or responder.

NITROGLYCERIN PATCHES People with a history of cardiac problems may have nitroglycerin patches on their chests. Since nitroglycerin can be absorbed by a responder, you should remove it with a gloved hand before defibrillation. Nicotine patches used to stop smoking look like nitroglycerin patches. In order to not waste time identifying patches, remove any patch you see on the person's chest.

HYPOTHERMIA Some people who have experienced hypothermia have been resuscitated successfully even after prolonged exposure. It will take longer to do your check, or assessment, of the person since you may have to check for signs of life and/or pulse for up to 30 to 45 seconds. If you do not feel a pulse, begin CPR until an AED becomes readily available. If the person is wet, dry his or her chest and attach the AED. If there still is no pulse, continue CPR. Follow local protocols as to whether additional shocks should be delivered. Continue CPR and protect the person from further heat loss. Do not

delay CPR or defibrillation to re-warm the person. Do not shake a hypothermia victim unnecessarily as this could result in ventricular fibrillation.

TRAUMA If a person is in cardiac arrest resulting from traumatic injuries, an AED may still be used. Defibrillation should be administered according to local protocols.

AED Maintenance

For defibrillators to perform optimally, they must be maintained like any other machine. AEDs require minimal maintenance. These devices have various self-testing features. However, it is important that operators are familiar with any visual or audible warning prompts the AED may have to warn of malfunction or a low battery. It is important that you read the operator's manual thoroughly and check with the manufacturer to obtain all necessary information regarding maintenance.

In most cases, if the machine detects any malfunction, you should contact the manufacturer. The device may need to be returned to the manufacturer for service. While AEDs require minimal maintenance, it is important to remember to—

- Follow the manufacturer's specific recommendations for periodic equipment checks.
- Make sure that the batteries have enough energy for one complete rescue. (Have a fully charged backup battery readily available.)
- Make sure that the correct defibrillator pads are in the package and are properly sealed.
- Check expiration dates on defibrillation pads and batteries. Replace as needed.
- After use, make sure that all accessories are replaced and that the machine is in proper working order.

If at any time the machine fails to work properly or warning indicators are recognized, discontinue use and contact the manufacturer immediately.

AED—CHILD

YOUNG CHILDREN AND THE CARDIAC CHAIN OF SURVIVAL

Sudden cardiac arrest can happen to anyone, at any time and not just to adults. While the incidence is relatively low compared with adults, cardiac arrest resulting from ventricular fibrillation (V-fib) does happen to young children and infants and is no less dramatic. The emotional trauma and devastation of the loss of a child to a family and community cannot be measured.

Most cardiac arrests in children are not sudden. The most common causes of cardiac arrest in children are—

- Airway and breathing problems.
- Traumatic injuries or an accident (e.g., automobile crashes, drowning, electrocution, poisoning).
- A hard blow to the chest (e.g., *commotio cordis*).
- Congenital heart disease.
- Sudden Infant Death Syndrome (SIDS).

V-fib is a type of abnormal heart rhythm that can occur in young children. Defibrillation is an electric shock that interrupts the heart's chaotic electrical activity during sudden cardiac arrest, most commonly caused by V-fib. The shock may help the heart restore its ability to function as a pump.

USING AN AED ON A CHILD (AGES 1 TO 8 OR WEIGHING LESS THAN 55 POUNDS)

Automated external defibrillators (AEDs) equipped with pediatric AED pads (Fig. 8-1) are capable of delivering lower levels of energy to a child between the ages of 1 and 8 or weighing less than 55 pounds.

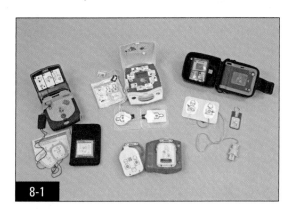

8-1

SOFT TISSUE INJURIES

INJURIES

The Leading Causes of Workplace Injury-Related Death

- Motor vehicle incidents
- Homicides
- Falls
- Accidents with machinery
- Injuries from falling objects
- Electrocutions

Workplace Injury Prevention Survey

Injuries do not just happen. For the most part, they are predictable and preventable. If you have not already done so, take the "Injury Prevention Survey" below. The survey will help make you more aware of conditions or situations around you that may lead to injury. It also may help you reduce your risk of injury, as well as your risk to others.

Check the "Yes" or "No" box next to the following questions:

Yes No

☐ ☐ Do you wear a safety belt when driving or riding in a company motor vehicle?

☐ ☐ Do you refrain from driving after drinking alcoholic beverages?

☐ ☐ Do the stairs where you work have handrails?

☐ ☐ Do you use a stepladder or sturdy stool to reach high, out-of-reach objects?

☐ ☐ Do you have adequate lighting in halls and stairways?

☐ ☐ Do you use good lifting techniques when lifting objects?

☐ ☐ Do you wear an appropriate helmet when using a bicycle, motorcycle or scooter?

☐ ☐ Do you wear a lifejacket when participating in work activities on or around the water?

☐ ☐ Do you wear safety protection (e.g., goggles, hearing protection) and follow equipment safety recommendations (e.g., Lock Out/Tag Out)?

If you answered "No" to two or more questions, consider reviewing the general safety tips in Appendix C.

SOFT TISSUE INJURIES— TYPES OF WOUNDS

Soft tissues are the layers of skin and the fat and muscle beneath the skin's outer layer. Any time the soft tissues are damaged or torn, the body is threatened. Injuries may damage the soft tissues at or near the skin's surface or deep in the body. Severe bleeding can occur at the skin's surface and under it, where it is harder to detect. Germs can get into the body through a scrape, cut, puncture or burn and cause infection. Burns are a special kind of soft tissue injury. Like other types of soft tissue injury, burns can damage the top layer of skin or the skin and the layers of fat, muscle and bone beneath.

Wounds are a physical injury involving a break in the layer(s) of the skin. Wounds are usually classified as either closed or open.

Closed Wound

In a closed wound (i.e., bruise, internal bleeding), the skin's surface is not broken and the damage to soft tissue and blood vessels happens below the surface, where bleeding sometimes occurs.

BRUISE (OR CONTUSION)

 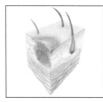

- Bleeding under the skin is caused by damage to soft tissues and blood vessels.
- The area may change from red to dark red or purple.
- A large or painful bruise may signal severe damage to deep tissues.

SIGNALS OF INTERNAL BLEEDING

- Tender, swollen, bruised or hard areas of the body, such as the abdomen
- Rapid, weak pulse
- Skin that feels cool or moist or looks pale or bluish
- Vomiting blood or coughing up blood
- Excessive thirst
- Becoming confused, faint, drowsy or unconscious

CARE FOR MINOR CLOSED WOUND

- Apply direct pressure.
- Elevate the injured body part if it *does not* cause more pain.
- Apply ice or a cold pack (Fig. 9-1).
  - When applying ice or a chemical cold pack, place a gauze pad, towel or other cloth between the source of cold and the person's skin.
  - Leave the ice or cold pack on for no more than 20 minutes. If continued icing is needed, remove the pack for 20 minutes and then replace it.

If the person complains of severe pain or cannot move a body part without pain or if you think the force that caused the injury was great enough to cause serious damage, seek medical care.

9-1

Open Wounds

In an open wound (i.e., cut, scrapes, lacerations, avulsions), the skin's surface is broken and blood may come through the tear in the skin.

ABRASION

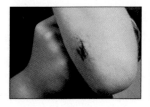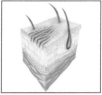

- Skin has been rubbed or scraped away; the area usually is painful (i.e., scrape, road rash, rug burn).

- Dirt and other matter can enter the wound; cleaning the wound is important to prevent infection.

LACERATION

- Cuts bleed freely, and deep cuts can bleed severely.
- Deep cuts can damage nerves, large blood vessels and other soft tissues.

AVULSION

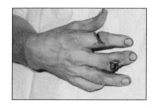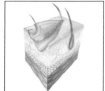

- A cut in which a piece of soft tissue or even part of the body, such as a finger, is torn loose or is torn off entirely (i.e., amputation).
- Often, deeper tissues are damaged, causing significant bleeding.

PUNCTURE

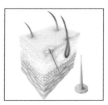

- Puncture wounds often do not bleed a lot and can easily become infected.
- Bleeding can be severe with damage to major blood vessels or internal organs.
- An embedded object in the wound should be removed only by advanced medical personnel.

CARE FOR A MINOR OPEN WOUND In minor open wounds, such as abrasions, there is only a small amount of damage and bleeding. To care for a minor wound, follow these general guidelines:

- Use a barrier between your hands and the wound. If readily available, put on disposable gloves and place a sterile dressing on the wound.
- Apply direct pressure for a few minutes to control any bleeding.
- Wash the wound thoroughly with soap and water. If possible, irrigate for about 5 minutes with clean, running tap water.
- Apply triple antibiotic ointment or cream to a minor wound if the person has no known allergies or sensitivities to the medication (Fig. 9-2).
- Cover the wound with a sterile dressing and bandage (or with an adhesive bandage) if it is still bleeding slightly or if the area of the wound is likely to come into contact with dirt or germs.

9-2

CARE FOR A MAJOR OPEN WOUND
- Control bleeding by placing a clean covering, such as a sterile dressing, over the wound and applying pressure.
- Apply a bandage snugly over the dressing.
- Call 9-1-1.
- Wash your hands immediately after completing care.

A Stitch in Time

It can be difficult to judge when a wound should receive stitches. One rule of thumb is that stitches are needed when edges of skin do not fall together, the laceration involves the face or when any wound is over $\frac{1}{2}$ inch long.

Stitches speed the healing process, lessen the chances of infection and improve the appearance of scars. They should be placed within the first few hours after the injury. Stitches in the face are often removed in less than a week. In joints, they are often removed after 2 weeks. Stitches on most other body parts require removal in 6 to 10 days. Some stitches dissolve naturally and do not require removal.

Jack Star/PhotoLink/Getty Images

The following major injuries often require stitches:
- Bleeding from an artery or uncontrolled bleeding
- Wounds that show muscle or bone, involve joints, gape widely or involve hands or feet
- Large or deep puncture wounds
- Large or deeply embedded objects
- Human or animal bites
- Wounds that, if left unattended, could leave conspicuous scars, such as those on the face

If you are caring for a wound and think it may need stitches, it probably does. Once applied, stitches can be easily cared for by following the health care provider's instructions. If the wound gets red or swollen or if pus begins to form, the health care provider should be notified.

Burns
- Burns are special types of soft tissue injuries.
- Burns can damage one or more layers of skin or the skin and the layers of fat, muscle and bone beneath.

Burns are caused by—
- Heat.
- Chemicals.
- Electricity.
- Radiation (sun).

TYPES OF BURNS

- **Superficial Burn** (first degree)
  - ○ Involves only the top layer of skin.
  - ○ The skin is red, dry, and usually painful and the area may swell.
  - Usually heals within a week without permanent scarring.

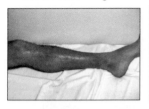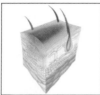

- **Partial Thickness** (second degree)
  - Involves the top layers of skin.
  - The skin is red; usually painful; has blisters that may open and weep clear fluid, making the skin appear wet; may appear mottled; and often swells.
  - Usually heals in 3 to 4 weeks and may scar.

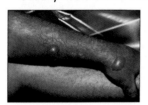

- **Full Thickness** (third degree)
  - May destroy all layers of skin and some or all of the underlying structures—fat, muscles, bones and nerves.
  - The skin may be brown or black (charred) with the tissue underneath sometimes appearing white.
  - Can either be extremely painful or relatively painless (if the burn destroys nerve endings).
  - Healing may require medical assistance; scarring is likely.

Critical Burns

Critical burns require medical attention. These burns are potentially life threatening, disfiguring and disabling. Even superficial burns can be critical if they affect a large area or certain body parts. You cannot judge a burn's severity by the pain that the burned person feels because nerve endings may be destroyed. You should always call 9-1-1 or the local emergency number if there are—

- Burns that cause troubled breathing.
- Burns covering more than one body part or a large surface area.
- Burns to the head, neck, hands, feet or genitals.
- Burns to the airway (burns to the mouth and nose may be a signal of this).
- Burns (other than a very minor one) to a child (younger than age 5) or an elderly person (older than age 60).
- Burns resulting from chemicals, explosions or electricity.

A critical burn can be life threatening and needs immediate medical attention. Call 9-1-1 or the local emergency number.

Care for Thermal (Heat) Burns

- Check the scene for safety.
- Stop the burning by removing the person from the source of the burn.
- Check for life-threatening conditions.
- Cool the burn with large amounts of cold running water until pain is relieved.
- Cover the burn loosely with a sterile dressing.
- Prevent infection.
- Take steps to minimize shock. Keep the person from getting chilled or overheated.
- Comfort and reassure the person.

Care for Chemical Burns

- The chemical will continue to burn as long as it is on the skin. You must remove the chemical from the body as quickly as possible.

- Flush the burn with large amounts of cool running water. Continue flushing the burn for at least 20 minutes or until emergency medical services (EMS) personnel arrive (Fig. 9-3).

- Dry chemicals that cause burns should be brushed off the skin using gloved hands before being flushed with tap water (under pressure), being careful not to get the chemical on yourself or the person (Fig. 9-4).

- If possible, have the person remove contaminated clothes to prevent further contamination while you continue to flush the area with cool running water.
- Be aware that chemicals can be inhaled, potentially damaging the airway or lungs.

Care for Electrical Burns

- Never go near a person with an electrical burn until you are sure the person is not still in contact with the power source.
- In the case of high-voltage electrocution, such as that caused by downed powerlines, call 9-1-1 or the local emergency number.
- Turn off the power at its source and care for any life-threatening conditions.
- An electrical burn may severely damage underlying tissue (Fig. 9-5).
- Electrocution can cause cardiac and breathing emergencies. Be prepared to give cardiopulmonary resuscitation or defibrillation. Care for shock and thermal burns.
- All people with electric shock require advanced medical care.

Care for Radiation (Sun) Burns

- Care for sunburns as you would any other burn.
- Cool the burn and protect the area from further damage by keeping it out of the sun.

When Caring for a Burn, DO NOT—

- Apply ice or ice water except on a small, superficial burn and then for no more than 10 minutes. Ice can cause the body to lose heat and further damages delicate tissue.
- Touch a burn with anything except a clean covering.
- Remove pieces of clothing that stick to the burned area.
- Try to clean a severe burn.
- Break blisters.
- Use any kind of ointment on a severe burn.

Preventing Burns

- Heat burns can be prevented by following safety practices that prevent fire and by being careful around sources of heat.
- Chemical burns can be prevented by following safety practices around all chemicals and by following manufacturers' guidelines whenever handling chemicals.
- Electrical burns can be prevented by following safety practices around electrical lines and equipment and by leaving outdoor areas when lightning could strike.
- Sunburn can be prevented by wearing appropriate clothing and using sunscreen. Sunscreen should have a sun protection factor (SPF) of at least 15.

Lightning

Traveling at speeds up to 300 miles per second, a lightning strike can hurl a person through the air. It can burn off clothes and can sometimes cause the heart to stop beating. The most severe lightning strikes carry up to 50 million volts of electricity, enough to serve 13,000 homes. Lightning can "flash" over a person's body or it can travel through blood vessels and nerves to reach the ground.

Besides burns, lightning can also cause nervous system damage, broken bones and loss of hearing or eyesight. People sometimes act confused and suffer memory loss. They may describe what happened as getting hit on the head or hearing an explosion.

Use common sense during thunderstorms. If you see a storm approaching in the distance, do not wait until you are soaked to seek shelter.

If a thunderstorm threatens, you should—

- Go inside a large building or home that has four solid walls and preferably electrical, telephone and plumbing lines, which aid in grounding the structure.
- Go inside a car and roll up the windows. Do not touch any of the car's metal framework when in the car.
- Stop swimming or boating as soon as you see or hear a storm because water conducts electricity.
- Stay away from the telephone, except in an emergency.
- Not shower or bathe during a thunderstorm.
- Stay away from telephone poles and tall trees if you are caught outside.
- Stay off hilltops; try to crouch down in a ravine or valley.
- Stay away from farm equipment and small metal vehicles, such as motorcycles, bicycles and golf carts.
- Avoid wire fences, wire clotheslines, some fishing rods, metal pipes and rails and other conductors.
- Stay several yards apart if you are in a group.

INFECTION PREVENTION

Harmful pathogens (germs) may enter the body through scrapes, cuts, punctures or burns and cause infection. Infection may develop within hours or days of an injury (Fig. 9-6A-B).

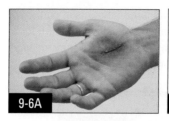

9-6A | 9-6B

How to Prevent an Infection

- Wash hands before and after caring for the wound, even if you wear gloves.
- Wash minor wounds with soap and water. If possible, irrigate with clean running water for about 5 minutes.
- Do not wash wounds that require medical attention unless instructed to do so by a medical professional.
- Cover the wound with a clean dressing and bandages, which should be changed daily.
- If an infection persists or worsens, have the person seek medical care.

Signals of an Infection

- The wound area becomes swollen and red.
- The area may feel warm or throb with pain.
- The area may discharge pus.
- Red streaks may develop around the wound.
- The person may develop a fever and feel ill.
- The person should seek medical attention for any developing infections.

CARE FOR SPECIAL SITUATIONS

Eye Injury

For an object embedded in the eye—

- **DO NOT** attempt to remove an object embedded in the eye.
- Place a sterile dressing around the object in the eye; stabilize the object, such as with a paper cup, for support.
- Bandage loosely and do not put pressure on the injured eye/eyeball (Fig. 9-7).
- Seek immediate medical attention.

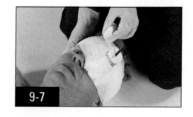

9-7

9-8

For small foreign bodies in the eye such as sand or other small debris—

- Tell the person to blink several times to try to remove the object.
- Gently flush the eye with water.
- Seek medical attention if the object remains. For chemicals in the eye—
- Flush the eye continuously with water for 10 minutes or until EMS personnel arrives. Always flush away from the uninjured eye (Fig. 9-8).

Embedded Objects

- Do not remove the object.
- Bandage bulky dressings around the object to keep it from moving.
- Bandage the dressing in place.
- Because shock is likely if bleeding is severe, give care to minimize shock.

Severed Body Parts

Take the following steps to care for a person suffering from a severed body part:

- Control bleeding.
- Wrap and bandage the wound to prevent infection.

9-9

- If bleeding is significant, give care to minimize shock.
- Wrap the severed body part in sterile gauze or a clean cloth.
- Place the severed body part in a plastic bag (Fig. 9-9).
- Put the plastic bag on ice (but do not freeze it) and keep it with the person.

Nosebleed

Take the following steps to control a nosebleed:

- Have the person sit leaning slightly forward.
- Pinch the nostrils together for about 10 minutes.
- Apply an ice pack to the bridge of the nose. If bleeding does not stop—
- Apply pressure on the upper lip just beneath the nose.
- Send someone to call 9-1-1 or the local emergency number if the person loses consciousness; position the person on the side to allow blood to drain from the nose.

Note: Seek medical attention if the bleeding persists or recurs or if the person says it results from high blood pressure.

After the bleeding stops—

- Have the person avoid rubbing, blowing or picking the nose, which could restart the bleeding.

Injuries to the Mouth and Teeth

If no serious head, neck or back injury is suspected—

- Rinse out the mouth with cold tap water if available.
- Have the person lean slightly forward or place the person on his or her side.
- Try to prevent the person from swallowing the blood, which may cause nausea or vomiting.
- Apply the dressing.
  - For inside the cheek—place folded sterile dressing inside the mouth against the wound.
  - For outside the cheek—apply direct pressure using a sterile dressing.
  - For the tongue or lips—apply direct pressure using a sterile dressing. Apply a cold compress to reduce swelling and ease pain.

TEETH KNOCKED OUT

- Rinse out the mouth with cold tap water if available.
- Have the person bite down on a rolled sterile dressing in the space left by the tooth (or teeth).
- Save any displaced teeth.
  - Carefully pick up the tooth by the crown (white part), not the root.
  - Rinse off the root of the tooth in water if it is dirty. Do not scrub it or remove any attached tissue fragments.
  - Place the tooth in milk, if possible, or water and keep it with the person.
- Get the person to a dentist as soon as possible (within 30 to 60 minutes after the injury).

Injuries to the Abdomen

If organs are exposed in an open wound—

- Do not apply pressure to organs or push them back inside.
- Keep the person lying down with his or her knees bent, if that position does not cause pain.
  - Put a folded blanket or pillow under the knees to support them in this position.
- Remove any clothing from around the wound.
- Loosely apply moist, sterile dressings or a clean cloth over the wound.
- Keep the dressing moist with warm water.
- Place a cloth over the dressing to keep organs warm.
- Give care to minimize shock.

If organs are not exposed—

- Keep the person lying down with knees bent, if that position does not cause pain.
  - Put a folded blanket or pillow under the knees to support the person in this position.
- Give care to minimize shock.

Animal Bites

If the bleeding is severe—

- Control bleeding.
- Call 9-1-1 or the local emergency number especially if you suspect the animal has rabies.
- Report the incident to the local animal-control officer or police.
- Check with a health care provider whether a tetanus booster may be necessary.

If the bleeding is minor—

- Control bleeding.
- Wash the wound with soap and warm water. If possible, irrigate with clean running tap water for about 5 minutes.
- Apply triple antibiotic ointment or cream if person has no known allergies or sensitivities to the medication.
- Cover the wound.
- Call 9-1-1 or the local emergency number if you suspect the animal has rabies.
- Report the incident to the local animal-control officer or police.
- Check with a heath care provider whether a tetanus booster may be necessary.

INJURIES TO MUSCLES, BONES AND JOINTS

Injuries to muscles, bones and joints can occur in the workplace as a result of accidents, such as falls, vehicle crashes, or forced impact with equipment or machinery.

TYPES OF MUSCLE, BONE AND JOINT INJURIES

- **Fracture**
  - ◦ Complete break, chip or crack in a bone (Fig. 10-1)
  - ◦ Caused by fall, blow or twisting movement
  - ◦ Open (open wound) or closed (skin not broken)
  - ◦ Can be life threatening if it involves a large bone, such as the thigh; severs an artery; or affects breathing

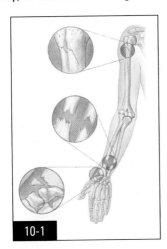

10-1

- **Dislocation**
  - ◦ Movement of a bone at a joint away from the normal position (Fig. 10-2).
  - ◦ More obvious than a fracture
  - ◦ Often forms a bump, ridge or hollow
- **Sprain**
  - ◦ Tearing of ligaments at a joint (Fig. 10-3A)
  - ◦ May swell and can involve fractures or dislocations
  - ◦ Most often occurs in the ankle, knee, wrist or finger joint

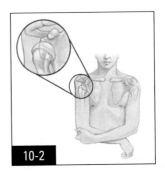

10-2

- **Strain**
  - ◦ Stretching and tearing of muscles or tendons (Fig. 10-3B)
  - ◦ Often caused by lifting or overwork
  - ◦ Usually involves muscles in the neck, back, thigh, shoulder or lower leg

It is difficult to know if a muscle, bone or joint injury is a fracture, dislocation, sprain or strain. It is not necessary to know the type of injury; the care given is the same whether the injury is a fracture, dislocation, sprain or strain. General care includes following **R.I.C.E.**—

- **R**est—Do not move or straighten the injured area.
- **I**mmobilize—Stabilize the injured area in the position found. Splint the injured part **ONLY** if the person must be moved and it does not cause more pain.
- **C**old—Fill a plastic bag or wrap ice with a damp cloth and apply ice to the injured area for periods of about 20 minutes. If continued icing is needed, remove the pack for 20 minutes and then replace it. Place a thin barrier between the ice and bare skin.
- **E**levate—**DO NOT** elevate the injured part if it causes more pain.

SIGNALS OF MUSCLE, BONE AND JOINT INJURIES

Always suspect a serious injury when any of the following signals are present:

- Significant deformity.

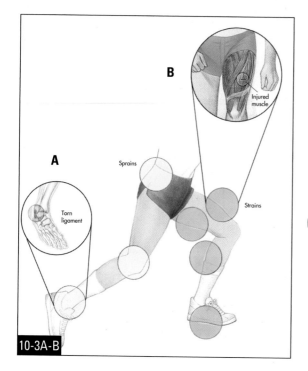

10-3A-B

- Bruising and swelling.
- Inability to use the affected part normally.
- Bone fragments sticking out of a wound.
- Person feels bones grating; person felt or heard a snap or pop at the time of injury.
- The injured area is cold and numb.
- Cause of the injury suggests that the injury may be severe.

SPLINTING

Splinting is a method of immobilizing an injured extremity and should be used ONLY if you have to move or transport a person to seek medical attention and if splinting does not cause more pain.

    If you have to splint—

- Splint the injury in the position in which you find it.
- Splint the injured area and the joints or bones above and below the injury site.
- Check for circulation (i.e., feeling, warmth and color) before and after splinting.

Methods of Splinting

- **Anatomic splints.** The person's body is the splint. For example, you can splint an arm to the chest or an injured leg to the uninjured leg.

- **Soft splints.** Soft materials such as a folded blanket, towels or pillows or a folded triangular bandage can be splint materials. A sling is a specific kind of soft splint that uses a triangular bandage tied to support an injured arm, wrist or hand.
- **Rigid splints.** Boards, folded magazines or newspapers or metal strips that do not have any sharp edges can serve as splints.
- **The ground.** An injured leg stretched out on the ground is splinted by the ground.

CARE FOR FOOT INJURIES

- Immobilize the ankle and foot by using a soft splint, such as a pillow or rolled blanket (Fig. 10-4).
- Do not remove the shoes.

10-4

CARE FOR LEG INJURIES

- Immobilize an injured leg by binding it to the uninjured leg (Fig. 10-5).

10-5

CARE FOR HAND AND FINGER INJURIES

- Apply a bulky dressing to the injured area.
- For a possible fractured or dislocated finger, tape the injured finger to a finger next to it (Fig. 10-6).

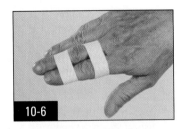
10-6

CARE FOR RIB/BREASTBONE FRACTURES

- Place a pillow or folded blanket between the injured ribs and the arm (Fig. 10-7).
- Bind the arm to the body to help support the injured area.

10-7

OPEN FRACTURE

An open fracture occurs when a bone is severely injured, causing the bone ends to tear through the skin and surrounding tissue (Fig. 10-8).

10-8

Care for an Open Fracture

- Call 9-1-1 or the local emergency number.
- Place sterile dressings around the open fracture as you would for an embedded object.
- Bandage the dressings in place around the fracture.
- Avoid moving the exposed bone and limb; this may cause the person a great deal of pain and may complicate recovery.

HEAD, NECK AND BACK INJURIES

Signals of Head, Neck and Back Injuries

- Change in consciousness
- Severe pain or pressure in the head, neck or back
- Tingling or loss of sensation in the hands, fingers, feet or toes
- Partial or complete loss of movement of any body part
- Unusual bumps or depressions on the head or over the neck and back
- Blood or other fluids in the ears or nose
- Heavy external bleeding of the head, neck or back
- Seizures
- Impaired breathing or vision as a result of injury
- Nausea or vomiting
- Persistent headache
- Loss of balance
- Bruising of the head, especially around the eyes and behind the ears

When to Suspect Head, Neck or Back Injuries

You should also suspect a head, neck or back injury if the person—
- Was involved in a motor vehicle crash.
- Was injured as a result of a fall from greater than a standing height.
- Reports of neck or back pain.
- Has tingling or weakness in the extremities.
- Is not fully alert.
- Appears to be intoxicated.
- Appears to be frail or over 65 years of age.

Care for Head, Neck and Back Injuries

- Call or have someone call 9-1-1 or the local emergency number.
- Minimize movement of the head, neck and back.
- Minimize movement by placing your hands on both sides of the person's head.
- Gently hold the person's head in line with the body.

- If the head is sharply turned to one side, do not try to align it with the body; support the head in the position you find it.
- Maintain an open airway.
- Monitor airway, breathing and signs of life.
- Control any external bleeding.
- Keep the person from getting chilled or overheated.

Wearing a helmet helps protect against head, neck or back injuries (Fig. 10-9A-C). However, if a person with a suspected head, neck or back injury is wearing a helmet, do not remove it unless it is necessary to assess the person's airway and you are specifically trained to do so. Minimize movement using the same technique as if there were no headgear.

10-9A

10-9B

10-9C

SKILL SHEET: ANATOMIC SPLINT

CHECK the scene for safety. **CHECK** the injured person following standard precautions. **CALL** 9-1-1 or the local emergency number if necessary. To **CARE** for a person who has an injured limb—

STEP 1: Obtain consent.
Support the injured area above and below the site of the injury.

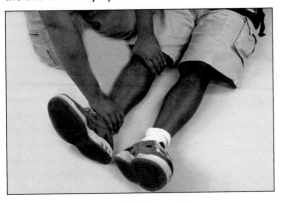

STEP 2: Check for feeling, warmth and color.

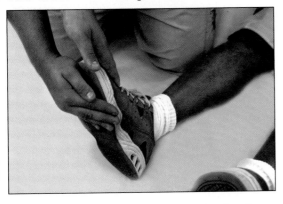

STEP 3: Place several folded triangular bandages above and below the injured area.

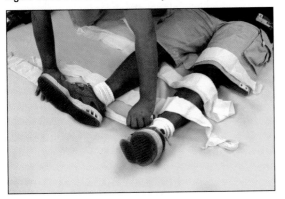

STEP 4: Place the uninjured area next to the injured area.

STEP 5: Tie triangular bandages securely.

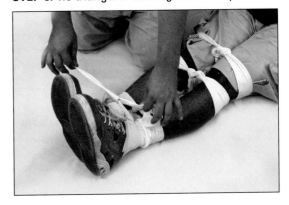

STEP 6: Recheck for feeling, warmth and color.

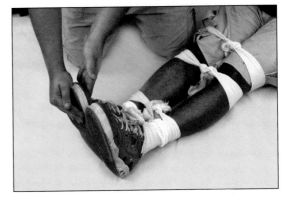

If you are not able to check warmth and color because a sock or shoe is in place, check for feeling.

SKILL SHEET: APPLYING A SOFT SPLINT

CHECK the scene for safety. **CHECK** the injured person following standard precautions. **CALL** 9-1-1 or the local emergency number if necessary. To **CARE** for a person who has an injured limb—

STEP 1: Obtain consent.

Support the injured area above and below the site of the injury.

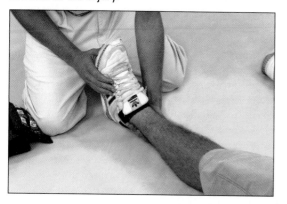

STEP 4: Gently wrap a soft object (a folded blanket or pillow) around the injured area.

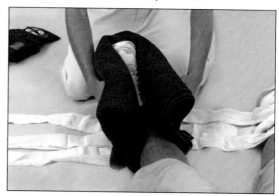

STEP 2: Check for feeling, warmth and color.

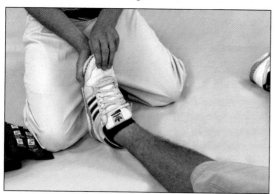

STEP 5: Tie triangular bandages securely with knots.

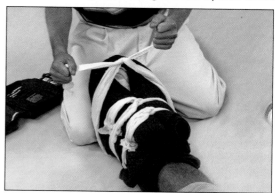

STEP 3: Place several folded triangular bandages above and below the injured area.

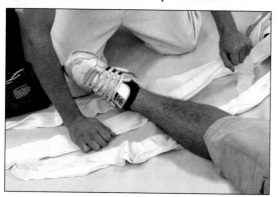

STEP 6: Recheck for feeling, warmth and color. If you are not able to check warmth and color because a sock or shoe is in place, check for feeling.

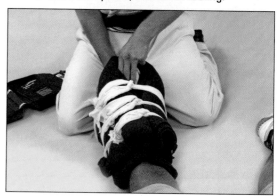

SKILL SHEET: APPLYING A SLING AND BINDER

CHECK the scene for safety. **CHECK** the injured person following standard precautions. **CALL** 9-1-1 or the local emergency number if necessary. To **CARE** for a person who has an injured limb—

STEP 1: Obtain consent.
Support the injured area above and below the site of the injury.

STEP 2: Check for feeling, warmth and color.

STEP 3: Place a triangular bandage under the injured arm and over the uninjured shoulder to form a sling.

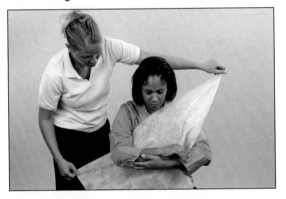

STEP 4: Tie the ends of the sling at the side of the neck.

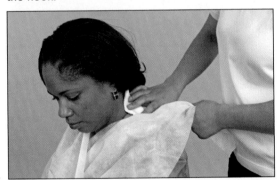

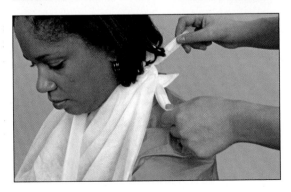

STEP 5: Bind the injured area to the chest with a folded triangular bandage.

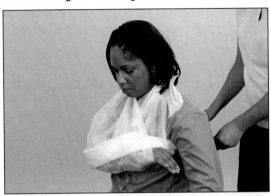

STEP 6: Recheck for feeling, warmth and color.

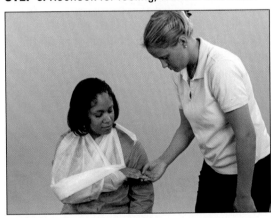

SKILL SHEET: APPLYING A RIGID SPLINT

CHECK the scene for safety. **CHECK** the injured person following standard precautions. **CALL** 9-1-1 or the local emergency number if necessary. To **CARE** for a person who has an injured limb—

STEP 1: Obtain consent.
Support the injured area above and below the site of the injury.

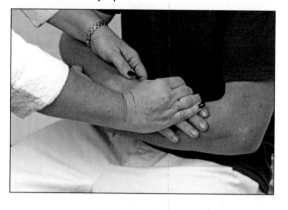

STEP 2: Check for feeling, warmth and color.

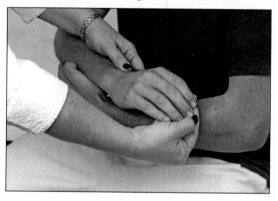

STEP 3: Place the rigid splint (board) under the injured area and the joints that are above and below the injured area.

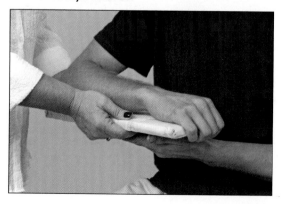

STEP 4: Tie several folded triangular bandages above and below the injured area.

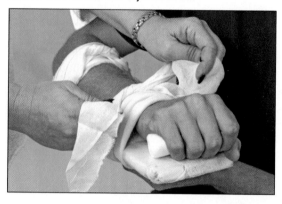

STEP 5: Recheck for feeling, warmth and color.

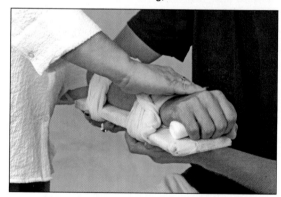

If a rigid splint is used on a forearm, you must also immobilize the elbow. Bind the arm to the chest using folded triangular bandages or apply a sling.

SUDDEN ILLNESS

You may not know the exact cause of a sudden illness, but this should not keep you from giving care. Generally, a person with sudden illness looks and feels ill. If you think something is wrong, check the person. A person may deny anything is seriously wrong. Do not be afraid to ask the person questions. The person's condition can worsen rapidly if he or she is not cared for. Sudden illness includes—

- Fainting.
- Diabetic emergency.
- Seizure.
- Stroke.
- Poisoning.
- Allergic reaction.

SIGNALS OF SUDDEN ILLNESS

When a person becomes suddenly ill, he or she usually looks and feels sick. Common signals include—

- Changes in consciousness, such as feeling light-headed or dizzy, or becoming unconscious.
- Nausea or vomiting.
- Difficulty speaking or slurred speech.
- Numbness or weakness.
- Loss of vision or blurred vision.
- Changes in breathing; the person may have trouble breathing or may not be breathing normally.
- Changes in skin color (pale, ashen or flushed skin).
- Sweating.
- Persistent pressure or pain.
- Diarrhea.
- Seizures.
- Paralysis or inability to move.
- Severe headache.

CARE FOR SUDDEN ILLNESS

- Do no further harm.
- Check the scene for clues about what might be wrong, then check the person.
- Call 9-1-1 or the local emergency number for life-threatening conditions.
- Monitor breathing and consciousness.
- Help the person rest in the most comfortable position.
- Keep the person from getting chilled or overheated.
- Reassure the person.
- Give any specific care needed.

FAINTING

When someone suddenly loses consciousness and then reawakens, he or she may simply have fainted. Fainting is not usually harmful and the person will usually quickly recover. Lower the person to the ground or other flat surface and position the person on his or her back. If possible, raise the person's legs about 12 inches. Loosen any tight clothing, such as a tie or collar. Check to make sure the person is breathing. Do not give the person anything to eat or drink. If the person vomits, position the person on his or her side.

DIABETIC EMERGENCY

People who are diabetic sometimes become ill because there is too much or too little sugar in their blood. Many diabetics use diet, exercise or medication to control their diabetes. You may know the person is a diabetic or the person may tell you he or she is a diabetic. Often, diabetics know what is wrong and will ask for something with sugar in it or may carry some form of sugar with them.

If the diabetic person is conscious and can safely swallow food or fluids, give him or her sugar, preferably in liquid form. Most fruit juices and nondiet soft drinks have enough sugar to be effective. You can also give table sugar dissolved in a glass of water. If the person's problem is low blood sugar, sugar will help quickly. If the problem is too much sugar, the sugar will not cause any further harm.

Always call 9-1-1 or the local emergency number if—

- The person is unconscious or about to lose consciousness.

- The person is conscious and unable to swallow.
- The person does not feel better within about 5 minutes after taking sugar.
- You cannot find sugar immediately. Do not spend time looking for it.

SEIZURES

Care for a person who has had a seizure the same way you would for any unconscious person. To protect the person from being injured, remove any nearby objects that might cause injury. Protect the person's head by placing a thin cushion under it. Folded clothing makes an adequate cushion. If there is fluid in the person's mouth, such as saliva, blood or vomit, roll him or her on one side so that the fluid drains from the mouth.

When the seizure is over, the person will usually begin to breathe normally. He or she may be drowsy and disoriented or unresponsive for a period of time. Check to see if the person was injured during the seizure. Be reassuring and comforting. If the seizure occurred in public, the person may be embarrassed and self-conscious. Ask bystanders not to crowd around the person. He or she will be tired and want to rest. Stay with the person until he or she is fully conscious and aware of his or her surroundings.

STROKE

- A stroke, also called a brain attack, is a blockage of blood flow to a part of the brain. It can cause permanent damage to the brain if the blood flow is not restored.
- A stroke can be caused by a blood clot or bleeding from a ruptured artery in the brain (Fig. 11-1).

Sudden Signals of Stroke

As with other sudden illnesses, the primary signals of a stroke or mini-stroke are a sudden change in how the body is working or feeling. This usually includes sudden weakness or numbness of the face, arm or leg. Usually, weakness or numbness occurs only on one side of the body. In addition, the person may—

- Have difficulty talking or being understood when speaking.

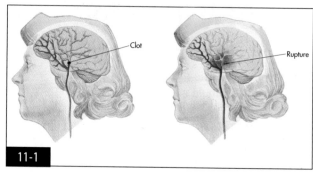

Clot

Rupture

11-1

- Have blurred or dimmed vision.
- Experience a sudden, severe headache; dizziness; or confusion.

F.A.S.T. Recognition of Stroke

For a Stroke Think F.A.S.T.
- **Face**—Weakness on one side of the face
  - Ask the person to smile; this will show if there is drooping or weakness in the muscles on one side of the face.
- **Arm**—Weakness or numbness in one arm
  - Ask the person to raise both arms to find out if there is weakness in the limbs.
- **Speech**—Slurred speech or trouble getting the words out
  - Ask the person to speak a simple sentence to listen for slurred or distorted speech (e. g., I have the lunch orders ready).
- **Time**—Time to call 9-1-1 if you see any of these signs
  - If a person has difficulty with any of these tasks or shows any other signals of a stroke, note the time that the signals began and call 9-1-1 right away.

POISONING

A poison is any substance that can cause injury, illness or death when introduced into the body (Fig. 11-2A-D).

If you suspect that a person is showing signals of poisoning, call the Poison Control Center at 800-222-1222. If the person is unconscious, there is a change in the level of consciousness or if another life-threatening condition is present, call 9-1-1 or the local emergency number.

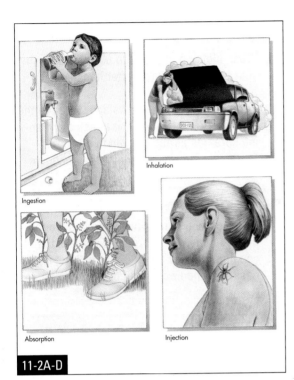

Ingestion

Inhalation

Absorption

Injection

11-2A-D

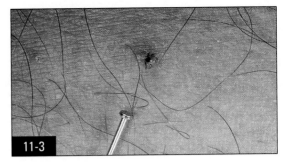

11-3

Care for Insect Stings

- Remove the stinger. Scrape it away from the skin with your fingernail or a plastic card, or use tweezers. If you use tweezers, grasp the stinger, not the venom sac.
- Wash the site with soap and water.
- Cover the site and keep it clean.
- Apply a cold pack to the area to reduce pain and swelling.
- Watch the person for signals of an allergic reaction.

Care for Tick Bites

- With a gloved hand, grasp the tick with fine-tipped, pointed, nonetched, nonrasped tweezers as close to the skin as possible and pull slowly (Fig. 11-3).
  - Do not try to burn the tick off.
  - Do not apply petroleum jelly or nail polish to the tick.
- Place the tick in a sealable container for analysis.
- Wash the bite area with soap and warm water.

- Apply antiseptic or triple antibiotic ointment.
- Wash your hands thoroughly.
- If rash, flu-like signals or joint pain appears, seek medical attention.
- If you cannot remove the tick or if its mouth-parts remain embedded, get the person medical care.

Care for Scorpion Stings and Spider Bites

If someone has been bitten by a scorpion, black widow spider or brown recluse spider—
- Wash the wound.
- Apply a cold pack to the site.
- Call 9-1-1 or the local emergency number.
- If it is available, give the person antivenin— a medication that blocks the effects of the spider's poisonous venom.

Care for Snake Bites

If someone has been bitten by a pit viper (such as a rattlesnake, copperhead or cotton mouth)—
- Call 9-1-1 or the local emergency number.
- Wash the wound.
- Keep the injured area still and lower than the heart.

If someone has been bitten by an elapid snake (such as a coral snake) (Fig. 11-4)—
- Call 9-1-1 or the local emergency number.
- Wash the wound.
- Apply an elastic roller bandage.
  For any snake bite, DO NOT—
- Apply ice.
- Cut the wound.
- Apply suction.
- Apply a tourniquet.
- Use electric shock.

11-4

David M. Dennis/Tom Stack & Associates

Care for Animal Bites

- Control bleeding first if the wound is bleeding seriously.
- Do not clean serious wounds; the wound will be cleaned at a medical facility.
- Call 9-1-1 or the local emergency number if the wound is bleeding seriously or you suspect the animal might have rabies.
- Wash minor wounds with soap and water.
- Control any bleeding.
- Apply a triple antibiotic ointment and a dressing.
- Watch for signals of infection.

Care for Marine Life Stings

For a jellyfish sting—
- Soak the area in vinegar.
  For a stingray sting—
- Immobilize the area.
- Soak the area in nonscalding hot water until pain goes away.
- Clean and bandage the wound.

Care for Exposure to Poisonous Plants

- Remove exposed clothing and wash the exposed area thoroughly with soap and water as soon as possible after contact with poisonous plants,

such as poison ivy, poison sumac and poison oak (Fig. 11-5A-C).
- Wash clothing exposed to plant oils. Wash your hands thoroughly after handling exposed clothing.
- Put a paste of baking soda and water on the area several times a day if a rash or weeping sore has already begun to develop.
- See a health care provider if the condition gets worse.

FILL IN THE BLANKS

1. If you know a person has a medical condition, you can give more specific care than if you do not know the cause of sudden illness. The medical conditions could include

   _____,
   _____,
   _____,
   _____,
   _____,
   or _____.

2. If a person vomits, position the person on his or her _____.

3. If a person faints and you do not suspect a head, neck or back injury, position the person on his or her _____ and elevate the _____ about 12 inches.

4. For a known diabetic emergency, give the person _____.

5. If poisoning were suspected, you would give the following care to the person

   _____.

11-5A

Ken Samuelson/Getty Images

11-5B

Larry West/Taxi/Getty Images

11-5C

Jeri Gleiter/Taxi/Getty Images

HEAT- AND COLD-RELATED EMERGENCIES

HEAT-RELATED EMERGENCIES

Heat-related emergencies are progressive conditions caused by overexposure to heat. If recognized in the early stages, heat-related emergencies can usually be reversed. If not recognized early, they may progress to heat stroke, a life-threatening condition.

There are three types of heat-related emergencies.

- **Heat cramps** are painful muscle spasms that usually occur in the legs and abdomen. Heat cramps are the least severe of the heat-related emergencies.
- **Heat exhaustion** (early stage) is an early indicator that the body's cooling system is becoming overwhelmed. Signals of heat exhaustion include—
  - Cool, moist, pale, ashen or flushed skin.
  - Headache, nausea, dizziness.
  - Weakness, exhaustion.
  - Heavy sweating.
- **Heat stroke** (late stage) is when the body's systems are overwhelmed by heat and stop functioning. Heat stroke is a life-threatening condition. Signals of heat stroke include—
  - Red, hot, dry (or moist) skin.
  - Changes in the level of consciousness.
  - Vomiting.

12-1

Care for Heat-Related Emergencies

Take the following steps to care for someone suffering from a heat-related emergency:
- Move the person to a cool place.
- Loosen tight clothing.
- Remove perspiration-soaked clothing.
- Apply cool, wet towels to the skin.
- Fan the person (Fig. 12-1).
- If the person is conscious, give small amounts of cool water to drink.

  If the person refuses water, vomits or starts to lose consciousness—
- Send someone to call 9-1-1 or the local emergency number.
- Place the person on his or her side.
- Continue to cool the person by using ice or cold packs on their wrists, ankles, groin and neck, and in the armpits.
- Continue to check signs of life (movement and breathing).

COLD-RELATED EMERGENCIES

It does not have to be extremely cold for someone to suffer a cold-related emergency, especially if the person is wet or if it is windy.

Hypothermia

Hypothermia occurs when the entire body cools because its ability to keep warm fails. The person will die if not given care.

SIGNALS OF HYPOTHERMIA
- Shivering, numbness, glassy stare
- Apathy, weakness, impaired judgment
- Loss of consciousness

Care for Hypothermia
- Gently move the person to a warm place.
- Monitor airway, breathing and circulation.
- Give rescue breathing or CPR if needed.
- Remove any wet clothing and dry the person.

12-2

- Handle the area gently; never rub the affected area.
- Warm gently by soaking the affected area in warm water (100°–105° F) until normal color returns and the area feels warm (Fig. 12-3A).
- Loosely bandage the area with dry, sterile dressings (Fig. 12-3B).
- If the person's fingers or toes are frostbitten, place dry, sterile gauze between them to keep them separated.
- Avoid breaking any blisters.
- Take precautions to prevent hypothermia.
- Call 9-1-1 or the local emergency number to seek emergency medical care as soon as possible.

- Warm the person by wrapping him or her in blankets or by putting dry clothing on the person (passive rewarming) (Fig. 12-2).
- If the person is alert, give him or her warm liquids to drink that do not contain alcohol or caffeine.
- Hot water bottles and chemical hot packs may be used when first wrapped in a towel or blanket before applying.
  - Do not warm the person too quickly, such as by immersing him or her in warm water. Rapid warming may cause dangerous heart rhythms.

Frostbite

Frostbite is the freezing of body parts exposed to the cold. Severity depends on the air temperature, length of exposure and the wind. Frostbite can cause the loss of fingers, hands, arms, toes, feet and legs.

SIGNALS OF FROSTBITE

- Lack of feeling in an affected area
- Skin that appears waxy, cold to the touch or discolored (flushed, white, yellow or blue)

CARE FOR FROSTBITE

- Get the person out of the cold.
- Do not attempt to rewarm the frostbitten area if there is a chance that it might refreeze or if you are close to a medical facility.

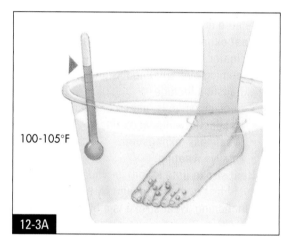
100-105°F
12-3A

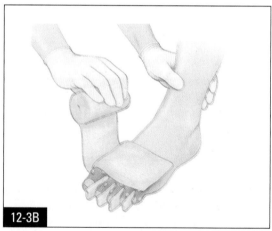
12-3B

ANATOMY OF A FIRST AID KIT

A well-stocked first aid kit is a handy thing to have. To be prepared for emergencies, keep a first aid kit in your home and in your automobile. Carry a first aid kit with you or know where you can find one. Find out the location of first aid kits where you work.

First aid kits come in many shapes and sizes. You can purchase one from **www.redcross.org** or your local America Red Cross chapter. Your local drug store may sell them. You may also make your own. Some kits are designed for specific activities, such as hiking, camping or boating. Whether you buy a first aid kit or put one together, make sure it has all the items you may need. Include any personal items, such as medications and emergency phone numbers, or other items your health care provider may suggest. Check the kit regularly. Make sure the flashlight batteries work. Check expiration dates and replace any used or out-of-date contents.

The American Red Cross recommends that all first aid kits include at a minimum the following:

- 2 absorbent compress dressings (5- × 9-inches)
- 25 adhesive bandages (assorted sizes)
- 1 adhesive cloth tape (10 yards × 1 inch)
- 5 triple antibiotic ointment packets (approximately 1 gram each)
- 5 antiseptic wipe packets
- 2 packets of aspirin (81 mg each)
- 1 blanket (space blanket)
- 1 breathing barrier (with one-way valve)
- 1 instant cold compress
- 2 pair of nonlatex gloves (size: large)
- 2 hydrocortisone ointment packets (approximately 1 gram each)
- Scissors
- 1 roller bandage (3-inches wide)
- 1 roller bandage (4-inches wide)
- 5 sterile gauze pads (3- × 3-inches)
- 5 sterile gauze pads (4- × 4-inches)
- Oral thermometer (non-mercury/nonglass)
- 2 triangular bandages
- Tweezers
- First aid instruction booklet

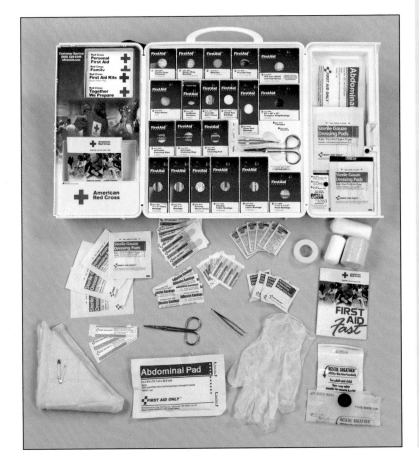

CHILD AND INFANT SAFETY CHECKLIST

"CHECK IT OUT!"

Directions: Use this checklist to spot dangers in your environment and check the box next to each statement if you follow the precaution. Each box that is not checked shows a possible danger to you and your family. Work with your family to remove dangers and make your home safer.

GENERAL SAFETY PRECAUTIONS

☐ Stairways and hallways are kept uncluttered and well lit. Safety gates are installed at all open stairways.

☐ Fire extinguishers, first aid kits and flash-lights are installed in areas where they might be needed.

☐ A planned emergency escape route with meeting location is in place and practiced.

☐ The hot water temperature is set below 120° F to prevent accidental scalding.

☐ Knives, guns, ammunition, power tools, razor blades, scissors and other objects that can cause injury are stored in locked cabinets or storage areas.

☐ A list of emergency phone numbers and medications taken (and by whom) is posted near telephones.

☐ Loose electrical cords are out of the flow of traffic. Multicord or octopus plugs (which can overheat) are not used.

☐ Space heaters and other electrical appli-ances are placed away from paper and walls.

☐ Electric cords and computer cables are not where people walk.

☐ Pesticides, detergents and other household chemicals are kept out of children's reach.

☐ Heavy objects are not placed on top of tall bookshelves or file cabinets.

☐ Smoke detectors are in working order. You have an emergency plan to use in case of fire, and your family practices this plan.

CHILD'S ROOM

☐ The crib mattress has a firm, flat, tight-fitting mattress.

☐ All soft bedding and pillow-like items have been removed from the crib before putting the infant down to sleep.

☐ The child's bed or crib is placed away from radiators and other hot surfaces.

☐ Crib slats are no more than 2 3/8-inches apart.

☐ Paint or finish on furniture and toys is non-toxic.

☐ Electric cords are kept out of child's reach.

☐ The child's clothing, especially sleepwear, is flame resistant.

PLAY AREAS

☐ Child guards are installed around fireplaces, wood-burning stoves, space heaters, radia-tors and hot pipes.

☐ Sharp edges of furniture are cushioned with corner guards or other material.

☐ Curtain cords and shade pulls are kept out of children's reach.

☐ Plastic bags are kept out of the reach of children and pets.

☐ Purses, handbags, briefcases, etc., including those of visitors, are kept out of children's reach.

☐ Windows and balcony doors have childproof latches.

☐ Balconies have protective barriers to prevent children from slipping through the bars.

☐ Smoke alarms are installed on each floor and especially near sleeping areas. Their batteries are changed in the spring and fall of each year.

☐ Space heaters are placed out of the reach of children and away from curtains.

- [ ] Flammable liquids, medicines, pesticides and other toxic materials are securely stored in their original containers and locked out of the reach of children.
- [ ] The toy box has ventilation holes, a sliding door or panel and a lightweight lid or a hinged lid with a support to hold it open in any position to which it is raised.

BATHROOM

- [ ] The bathroom door is kept closed.
- [ ] Children are ALWAYS supervised when they are around water (tub, basin, toilet) and/or electricity.
- [ ] Medicines and cleaning products are in containers with safety caps and locked away in cabinets with safety latches.
- [ ] Hair dryers and other appliances are stored away from sinks, tubs and toilets.
- [ ] The water is set at a safe temperature. (A setting of 120° F [49° C] or less prevents scalding from tap water in sinks and in tubs. Let the water run for 3 minutes before testing it.)
- [ ] The toilet seat and lid are kept down when the toilet is not in use.
- [ ] The bottom of the tub/shower has nonslip surfacing.

KITCHEN

- [ ] Small appliances are kept unplugged when not in use and stored out of the reach of children.
- [ ] Hot liquids and foods are handled with easily available potholders, the stove's back burners are used and pot handles are turned to the back of the stove.
- [ ] Highchairs are placed away from the stove and other hot objects. An infant is not left alone in a highchair and the infant is always secured by using all safety straps.

- [ ] Stove and sink areas are well lit and there is ample countertop space.
- [ ] The kitchen is equipped with a stepladder or stepstool so you do not have to use a chair to reach overhead objects.
- [ ] Cabinets with cleaning products in them are locked up.

CAR SAFETY

- [ ] All infants and children ride in approved safety seats.
- [ ] The infant's car seat faces the rear of the vehicle unless the infant is at least 20 pounds AND 1 year of age.
- [ ] A rear-facing car safety seat is NEVER placed in the front passenger seat. The car safety seat meets the following guidelines:
  - [ ] Infant or child's car safety seat
  - [ ] Fits in the vehicle appropriately
  - [ ] Fits the child properly
  - [ ] Is used correctly
  - [ ] Has never been in a crash

OUTSIDE

- [ ] Trash is kept in tightly covered containers.
- [ ] Sandboxes are covered when not in use.
- [ ] Seatbelts and properly attached car seats are used for all trips in the car (truck, van, etc.).
- [ ] Swimming pools and hot tubs are completely enclosed with a barrier (i.e., a locked fence and locked safety cover, respectively) and young children are kept away from them unless there is constant adult supervision.

For product safety information, call the U.S. Consumer Product Safety Commission's toll-free "Consumer Hotline" at 800-638-2772 or visit their Web site at **www.cpsc.gov**. Hearing- and speech-impaired callers can dial 800-638-8270.

INJURY PREVENTION

VEHICLE SAFETY

The following statements represent an awareness of vehicle safety that can reduce your chances, and the chances of others, of injury in a vehicle crash.

- When riding in a motor vehicle, buckle up. Wearing a safety belt is the easiest and best action you can take to prevent injury in a motor-vehicle collision. Always wear a safety belt, including a shoulder restraint, when riding in the front or back seats.
- Do not drink and drive. Plan ahead to find a ride or take a cab or public transportation if you are going to a party where you may drink alcohol. If you are with a group, have a designated driver who agrees not to drink on this occasion.

Using car safety seats and vehicle restraints properly is very important for infants and children. Safety restraints, properly used, help prevent death and injury.

- Infants and children should always ride in child safety seats approved by the National Highway Traffic Safety Administration of the U.S. Department of Transportation.
- The infant's car seat should face the rear of the vehicle until the infant weighs at least 20 pounds AND is 1 year of age.
- Infants who weigh 20 pounds before age 1 should ride facing the rear in a convertible seat or infant seat approved for higher weights until 1 year of age.
- A rear-facing car safety seat must NEVER be placed in the front passenger seat. Assume that all vehicles have air bags, which are dangerous to children and infants in the front seat.
- In rear-facing car safety seats for infants, shoulder straps must be at **or below** the infant's shoulders. The harness must be snug and the car safety seat retainer clip should be positioned at the midpoint of the infant's chest, not at the abdomen or the neck.
- A belt-positioning booster seat should be used when the child has outgrown a con-

vertible safety seat but is too small to fit properly in a vehicle safety belt.
- When the vehicle safety belt fits properly, the lap belt lies low and tight across the child's hips (not the abdomen) and the shoulder belt lies flat across the shoulder, away from the neck and face. Usually a child who weighs 80 pounds and is 5 feet in height can fit appropriately in a vehicle safety belt.

FIRE SAFETY TIPS

If a fire occurs, would you know what to do? Follow these safety guidelines to protect those you care about.

Install and Maintain Smoke Alarms

- Smoke alarms save lives by giving you more time to escape safely. Install them on every level of your home, especially near sleeping areas.
- Test and vacuum smoke alarms monthly. (Dust can impair their effectiveness.)
- Replace smoke alarm batteries when you change the time on your clocks each spring and fall.

Plan and Practice an Escape Plan

- Plan two ways out of every room (not including elevators).
- Choose a meeting place outside where everyone should gather in case of a fire.
- Practice your plan every month to make sure everyone knows what to do.

Learn How to Use a Fire Extinguisher

- Place fire extinguishers at every level of your home, especially in the kitchen, basement and garage. These areas have the greatest danger of a chemical or electrical fire.
- Practice how to use the fire extinguisher.
- Check them monthly to make sure they are in proper working condition by following the manufacturer's guidelines.

Make Sure Your Address Is Visible

- Make sure your house or business number is visible from the street in a well-lit area so it can be seen at night and the fire department can easily find you, if necessary.
- Check with your local fire department if you need an address sign made for you.

Use Electrical Appliances Safely

- Check lamps and ceiling fixtures to make sure wiring is intact.
- If an appliance smokes or smells, unplug it or turn it off immediately.
- Examine electrical cords before use, and replace any that are frayed or cracked.
- Do not overload electrical outlets.
- Use safety plugs to prevent electrical fires.

If a Fire Does Occur

- If you must get through smoke to escape, keep low to the floor.
- The cleanest air will be 12 to 14 inches above the floor.
- Crawl on your hands and knees to get to the nearest safe exit.
- If possible, cover your mouth and nose with a damp cloth or handkerchief.
- IF THERE IS A FIRE, NEVER GO BACK INSIDE THE HOUSE TO GET ANYTHING.

Do Not Play with Fire

- Teach children that matches and lighters are not toys and are dangerous.
- Store lighters and matches where a child cannot get to them.
- Keep burning candles away from infants and children.

A HOTEL ESCAPE PLAN COULD SAFE YOUR LIFE

- Locate the fire exits and fire extinguishers on your floor.
- If you hear an alarm while in your room, feel the door first and do not open it if it is hot.
- Do not use the elevator.
- If the hall is relatively smoke free, use the stairs to exit. If the hall is filled with smoke, crawl to the exit. If you cannot get to the exit, return to your room.
- Turn off the ventilation system, stuff door cracks and vents with wet towels and call the front desk or the fire department to report the fire and your location.

SAFETY AT WORK

To improve safety at work, you should be aware of—

- Fire evacuation procedures.
- How to activate your emergency response team and how to call 9-1-1 or the local emergency number.
- The location of the nearest fire extinguisher and first aid kit.
- How to use recommended safety equipment and follow safety procedures if you work in an environment where hazards exist.
- Take workplace safety training seriously.

If you work in an environment where hazards exist, wear recommended safety equipment and follow safety procedures. Both employers and employees must follow safety rules issued by the Occupational Safety and Health Administration.

Whenever you operate machinery or perform an activity that may involve flying particles, you should wear protective eyewear, such as goggles. Inspect mechanical equipment and ladders periodically to ensure that they are in good working order. Check for worn or loose parts that could break and cause a mishap. Before climbing a ladder, place its legs on a firm, flat surface and have someone anchor it while you climb.

Take workplace safety training seriously. Ask your employer about first aid and cardiopulmonary resuscitation refresher courses.

Have your own personal workplace disaster supply kit. For the workplace, where you might be confined for several hours, or perhaps overnight, the following supplies are recommended:

- Flashlight with extra batteries
- Battery-powered radio
- Food
- Water

- Medications
- First aid supplies
- Tools and supplies

SAFETY AT HOME

Taking the following steps will help make your home a safer place.

- Post emergency numbers—9-1-1 or the local emergency number, Poison Control center and physician, as well as other important numbers—near every phone.
- Make sure that stairways and hallways are well lit.
- Equip stairways with handrails and use non-slip tread or securely fastened rugs.
- Secure rugs to the floor with double-sided tape.
- If moisture accumulates in damp spots, correct the cause of the problem. Clean up spills promptly.
- Keep medicines and poisonous substances separate from each other and from food. They should be out of reach of children and in secured cabinets.
- Keep medicines in their original containers, with safety caps.
- Keep your heating and cooling systems and all appliances in good working order. Check heating and cooling systems annually before use.
- Read and follow manufacturers' instructions for electrical tools, appliances and toys.
- Turn off the oven and other appliances when not using them. Unplug certain appliances, such as an iron, curling iron, coffee maker or portable heater, after use.
- Make sure that your home has at least one working, easily accessible fire extinguisher and that everyone knows how to use it.
- Have an emergency fire escape plan and practice it.
- Try crawling around your home to see it as an infant or young child sees it. You may become aware of unsuspected hazards.
- Turn pot handles toward the back of the stove.
- Ensure that cords for lamps and other items are not placed where someone can trip over them.

This list does not include all the safety measures you need to take in your home. If young children or elderly or ill individuals live with you, you will need to take additional steps, depending on the individual characteristics of your home.

POISON PREVENTION

- Poison-proof any area where children or infants may be present.
- Close any container of a substance that could harm a child or infant as soon as you have finished using it.
- Keep pills in their original container.
- Keep all medicines, iron-containing vitamins and household cleaning products out of reach and out of sight of children.
- Never keep medicines on a countertop or bedside table.
- Follow medicine label directions carefully to avoid accidental overdoses or misdoses that could result in accidental poisoning.
- Keep containers that use cake deodorizers (such as diaper pails) securely closed.
- Keep poisonous plants out of children's reach.
- Never refer to medicine as candy.
- Keep handy the number of the Poison Control Center: 800-222-1222.
- Do not operate portable generators inside a workspace or an enclosed building.

CARBON MONOXIDE POISONING PREVENTION

- Buy and install carbon monoxide (CO) detectors/alarms.
  - Install a CO detector/alarm in the hallway near every separate sleeping area of the home. Make sure the detector/alarm cannot be covered up by furniture or draperies. Follow manufacturer's instructions regarding the specific location where to install it. Avoid corners (where air does not circulate).
  - CO detectors/alarms are available for boats and recreational vehicles and should be used. The Recreational Vehicle Industry Association requires CO detectors/alarms

to be installed in motor homes and in towable recreation vehicles that have a generator or are prepped for a generator.

- Before buying a CO alarm, make sure it is listed with Underwriters Laboratories, standard 2034, or that there is information on the package or owner's manual that says that the detector/alarm meets the requirements of the IAS 6-96 standard.

- Prevent CO poisoning.
  - Make sure appliances are installed according to manufacturer's instructions and local building codes.
  - Have the heating system inspected and serviced annually.
  - Burn charcoal only outdoors, never inside a home, garage, vehicle or tent.
  - Do not use portable fuel-burning camping equipment inside a home, garage, vehicle or tent.
  - Always turn off any gas-powered engine inside an attached garage or basement.
  - Always refer to the owner's manual when performing minor adjustments or servicing fuel-burning appliances and get help from a professional if you are unsure how to service such equipment.
  - Do not use gas appliances such as ranges, ovens or clothes dryers for heating your home.
  - If you use a fuel-burning appliance for approved indoor uses, make sure it is vented to the outdoors following manufacturer's instructions.
  - Install and use an exhaust fan vented to outdoors over gas stoves.
  - Open flues when fireplaces are in use.
  - Choose properly sized wood-burning stoves that are certified to meet Environmental Protection Agency emission standards.
  - Have a trained professional inspect, clean and tuneup central heating systems annually.

SUN EXPOSURE

To prevent sunburn and other health problems, protect infants and children from the sun. Help children learn good habits for their future years.

- Schedule outdoor activities before 10 a.m. and after 3 p.m. (standard time) or before 11 a.m. and after 4 p.m. (daylight savings time).
- Monitor the daily UV Index forecasts for your area (on the Web at **www.epa.gov**, on television or in newspapers), and plan indoor activities on days of high sun intensity.
- Teach children how to find good shade areas.
- Keep infants and small children in the shade while outdoors.
- Plan trips to parks and places where adequate shade is available.
- Plant shade trees on school or childcare center property.
- Use portable shade structures, such as umbrellas, tents and tarps.
- Build permanent shade structures, such as porches, picnic shelters and fabric shade canopies.
- Include shade coverings in the design of playground equipment and recreational areas.
- Use a sunscreen with a sun protection factor of at least 15 that blocks both UVA and UVB rays.
- Use a broad-brimmed hat to shade an infant or child's head, face, scalp, ears and neck from the sun.
- Use sunglasses to protect an infant or child's eyes. Excessive sun exposure can cause cataracts later in life.

WATER SAFETY TIPS

- Learn to swim. The best thing anyone can do to stay safe in and around the water is to learn to swim.
  - The American Red Cross has swimming courses for people of any age and swimming ability. Contact your local Red Cross about available classes.
- Always swim with a buddy; never swim alone.
- Swim only in areas supervised by a lifeguard.
- Obey all rules, signs and lifeguard instructions.
- Children or inexperienced swimmers should take precautions, such as wearing a U.S.

Coast Guard-approved personal floatation device around the water.

- Watch out for the "dangerous too's":
  - Too tired
  - Too cold
  - Too far from safety
  - Too much sun
  - Too much strenuous activity
- Set water safety rules for the whole family based on swimming abilities (for example, inexperienced swimmers should stay in water less than chest deep).
- Be knowledgeable of the water environment you are in and its potential hazards, such as deep and shallow areas, currents, depth changes, obstructions and where the entry and exit points are located. The more informed you are, the more aware you will be of hazards and safe practices.
- Pay attention to local weather conditions and forecasts. Stop swimming at the first indication of bad weather.
- Use a feet-first entry when entering the water. Enter head-first only when the area is clearly marked for diving and has no obstructions.
- Do not mix alcohol and swimming.
  - Alcohol impairs your judgment, balance and coordination; affects your swimming and diving skills; and reduces your body's ability to stay warm. It also reduces your ability to supervise infants and children.
- Know how to prevent, recognize and respond to water emergencies.
- Always model safe behavior.

If you have a residential pool, you will need to take additional steps, such as—

- Learn to swim—and be sure everyone in the household knows how to swim.
- Never leave a child unattended who may gain access to any water. Even a small amount of water can be dangerous to young children.
- Teach your child not to go near the water without you; the pool area is off limits without adult supervision.
- Adult supervision is essential. Adult eyes must be on the child at all times.
- Enclose the pool completely with a fence with vertical bars (so that it is not easy to climb) that has a self-closing, self-latching gate. Openings in the fence should be no more than 4 inches wide. The house should not be part of the barrier. If the house is part of the barrier for an existing pool, an additional fence should be installed between the house and the pool, and the doors and windows leading from the house to the pool should remain locked and be protected with an alarm that produces sound when the door is unexpectedly opened.
- Post the rules for your pool and enforce them without exception. For example, never allow anyone to swim alone, do not allow bottles or glass around the pool, do not allow running or pushing and do not allow diving unless your pool meets the safety standards.
- Post depth markers and "No Diving" signs, as appropriate. Use a buoyed line to show where the depth changes from shallow to deep. Limit nonswimmer activity to shallow water.
- Never leave furniture or toys near the fence that would enable a child to climb over the fence.
- Keep toys away from the pool and out of sight when the pool is not in use. Toys can attract young children into the pool.
- Pool covers should always be completely removed prior to pool use and completely secured when in place.
- Have an emergency action plan to address potential emergencies.
- Post CPR and first aid instructions.
- Post the emergency telephone number for the emergency medical services system by your telephone. Keep a telephone near the pool or bring a fully charged cordless or mobile phone poolside. Also post your address and the nearest cross street so that anyone can read them to an emergency dispatcher.
- Always keep basic lifesaving equipment by the pool and know how to use it. A reaching pole; rope; and flotation devices, such as ring buoys, rescue tubes and life jackets, are recommended. A well-stocked first aid kit should also be available. Store the safety gear in a consistent, prominent,

easily accessible location. A "safety post" may be used.

- If a child is missing, check the pool first. Go to the edge of the pool and scan the entire pool-bottom surface, as well as the surrounding pool area.
- Keep the pool water clean and clear. Water should be chemically treated and tested regularly. If you cannot clearly see the bottom of the deep end, close the pool. Contact a local pool store or health department for information or instruction.
- Store pool chemicals—chlorine, soda ash, muriatic acid, test kits—in childproof containers and out of children's reach. Clearly label the chemicals. Follow manufacturer's directions and safety instructions.
- Consult the National Spa and Pool Institute, state law and local building codes for pool dimension guidelines to help you establish rules for your pool to ensure safe diving activities.
- Make sure your homeowner's insurance policy covers the pool.

BEACH SAFETY

- Protect your skin.
- Drink plenty of water regularly and often even if you do not feel thirsty.
- Watch for signals of heat stroke.
- Wear eye protection.
- Wear foot protection.

BOATING SAFETY

- Learn to swim.
- Remember, alcohol and boating do not mix.
- Look for the label: Use Coast Guard-approved life jackets for yourself and your passengers when boating and fishing.
- Develop a float plan.
- Find a boating course in your area—these courses teach about navigation rules; emergency procedures; and the effects of wind, water conditions and weather.
- Watch the weather.

RECREATIONAL SAFETY TIPS

Bicycle Safety

- Many bicycle injuries can be prevented by wearing a helmet. Always wear a correctly fitting helmet when riding.
- Be sure that helmets meet standards set by the U.S. Consumer Product Safety Commission (CPSC), the Snell Memorial Foundation or the American Society for Testing and Materials. Look for a label or a sticker on the box or inside the helmet indicating that it meets the above standards.
- Wear closed shoes when riding a bike.
- Make sure your bike has good brakes, a front light and effective reflecting material.
- Ride only in safe areas and at safe times.
- Make sure the bike is the correct size for the rider.
- Learn about bicycle etiquette, laws and safe riding practices.

Hiking and Camping Safety

- If you have any medical conditions, discuss your plans with your health care provider and get approval before departing.
- Review the equipment, supplies and skills that you will need. Consider what emergencies could arise and how you would deal with those situations.
  - What if you got lost or were unexpectedly confronted by an animal?
  - What if someone became ill or injured?
  - What kind of weather might you encounter?
- Make sure you have the skills you need for your camping or hiking adventure. You may need to know how to read a compass, erect a temporary shelter or give first aid.
- If your trip will be strenuous, get into good physical condition before setting out. If you plan to climb or travel to high altitudes, make plans to adjust to the altitude. It is safest to hike or camp with at least one companion. If you will be entering a remote area, your group should have a minimum of four people; this way, if one is hurt, another can stay with the person while two go for help. If you will be going into an area that is

unfamiliar to you, take along someone who knows the area or at least speak with those who do before you set out.

- Pack emergency signaling devices and know ahead of time the location of the nearest telephone or ranger station in case an emergency does occur on your trip.
- Leave a copy of your itinerary with a responsible person. Include such details as the make, year and license plate number of your car, the equipment you are bringing; the weather you have anticipated; and when you plan to return.
- Always allow for bad weather and for the possibility that you may be forced to spend a night outdoors unexpectedly.
- It is a good idea to assemble a separate "survival pack" for each hiker to have at all times. In a small waterproof container, place a pocketknife, compass, whistle, space blanket, nylon filament, water-purification tablets, matches and candle. With these items, the chances of being able to survive in the wild are greatly improved.

SAFETY OUTDOORS

Protect Yourself From Insects

- Wear a light-colored long-sleeved shirt, long pants and a hat.
- Secure your clothing to prevent insects from getting underneath.
- Avoid underbrush and tall grass when hiking.
- Use an insect repellent and follow the directions for use. Be sure to read cautionary statements on the label. Follow special precautions when using on children.
- After being outdoors for a long period, inspect yourself for ticks or have someone else do it. Shower immediately after coming indoors.
- If you have pets that go outdoors, use a repellent made for that type of pet and apply, according to the label. Be sure to check your pet for ticks often.

Playground Safety

Make it a top priority to keep children's play areas safe.

SUPERVISION IS ALWAYS A MUST!

- Adult supervision is always needed on the playground.
  - Watch for potential hazards and keep areas free of glass, sharp items and other dangerous items.
  - Observe children playing and intervene when necessary.
  - Avoid having children wear clothing with drawstrings around the neck.

AGE MATTERS FOR SAFE PLAY

- Preschoolers, ages 2 to 5, and children, ages 5 to 12, need separate play areas and different equipment.

SOFTEN THE POSSIBLE FALLS Most playground injuries are caused by falls. Playground surfaces should contain material that meets or exceeds the critical height requirement as identified by the CPSC (**www.cpsc.gov**). Check with the manufacturer/supplier and the governing body of your area.

Below are examples of some common materials:
- Wood chips/engineered wood fibers
- Mulch
- Pea gravel
- Sand
- Synthetic materials:
  - Poured-in-place
  - Rubber mats

EQUIPMENT SAFETY

- Equipment needs to be anchored safely in the ground.
- All equipment pieces should be in good working order, so that—
  - S-hooks are completely closed.
  - Bolts are not protruding.
  - There are no exposed footings.

INCIDENT STRESS

An emergency involving a serious injury or death is a critical incident. The acute stress it causes for staff, especially the responder, may overcome a person's ability to cope. This is often called incident stress, which may have a powerful impact. If not appropriately managed, this acute stress may lead to a serious condition called post-traumatic stress syndrome.

A person suffering from incident stress may become anxious and depressed and be unable to sleep. He or she may have nightmares, nausea, restlessness, loss of appetite and other problems. Some effects may appear right away and others only after days, weeks or even months have passed. People suffering from incident stress may not be able to perform well in their job.

SIGNALS OF INCIDENT STRESS REACTIONS

- Confusion
- Lower attention span
- Poor concentration
- Denial
- Guilt
- Depression
- Anger
- Change in interactions with others
- Increased or decreased eating
- Uncharacteristic, excessive humor or silence
- Unusual behavior

GUIDELINES TO COPE WITH INCIDENT STRESS

This type of stress requires professional help to prevent post-traumatic stress syndrome. Other things the person may do to help reduce stress include using relaxation techniques, eating a balanced diet, avoiding alcohol and drugs, getting enough rest and participating in some type of physical exercise or activity.

SUBSTANCE ABUSE

A wide range of drugs and other substances are abused in our society, with a wide range of psychological and physiological effects. Your goal is not to try to diagnose a clear case of a person being under the influence of a drug or other substance. The goal of care is to recognize a possible overdose or other problem requiring medical attention or other professional help. Do not be judgmental or assume an illegal drug is involved. Instead, treat the situation like any other case of sudden illness.

WHAT TO LOOK FOR

- Behavioral changes not otherwise explained
- Sudden mood changes
- Restlessness, talkativeness, irritability
- Altered consciousness
- Slurred speech, poor coordination
- Moist or flushed skin
- Chills, nausea, vomiting
- Dizziness, confusion
- Irregular pulse
- Irregular breathing
- Loss of consciousness

WHAT TO DO

CHECK the scene for safety. **CALL** the Poison Control Center (800-222-1222) and follow its directions if you have reason to suspect a substance was taken. **CALL** 9-1-1 or the local emergency number if—

- The person is unconscious, confused or seems to be losing consciousness.
- The person has trouble breathing or is breathing irregularly.
- The person has persistent chest pain or pressure.
- The person has pressure or pain in the abdomen that does not go away.
- The person is vomiting blood or passing blood.
- The person has a seizure, severe headache or slurred speech.
- The person engages in violent behavior.
- You are unsure what to do.
- You are unsure about the severity of the problem.

CARE for someone you suspect is under the influence of a substance by taking the following steps:

1. Try to learn from others what substance may have been taken.
2. Calm and reassure the person.
3. Monitor the airway, breathing and circulation (**ABCs**).
4. To minimize shock, keep the person from getting chilled or overheated.

SPECIAL SITUATIONS AND CIRCUMSTANCES

CARING FOR CHILDREN

Children have unique needs that require special care. Caring for a child requires that a responder recognize the child's fear and anxiety.

There are important characteristics to remember when checking a child:

- Obtain consent from a parent or guardian if present.
- Observe the child. Do not just rush up and touch the child.
- Remain calm. Children will be more upset if you are excited.
- Talk clearly and simply.
- Do not separate a child from loved ones, such as parents or guardians. Care for the child in the parent/guardian's arms if possible.
- Gain trust through actions.
- Explain what you are doing.

Interacting with Parents and Caregivers

If the family is excited or agitated, the child is likely to be too. When you can calm the family, the child will often calm down as well. Remember to get consent to give care from any adult responsible for the child when possible. Any concerned adults need your support. Remember to observe the whole situation and ask questions to see if there may be any special needs to consider.

Some children and adults are dependent on technology, such as tracheotomy tubes, mechanical ventilators, feeding tubes or pacemakers. When caring for someone with special needs, it is important to ask if he or she has an emergency information form summarizing vital information, including allergies and other medical problems or issues.

Child Abuse

At some point, you may encounter a situation involving an injured child in which you have reason to suspect child abuse. *Child abuse* is the physical, psychological or sexual assault of a child resulting in injury and emotional trauma.

Child abuse involves an injury or a pattern of injuries that do not result from an accident. Suspect child abuse if the child's injuries cannot be logically explained or if a parent or guardian gives an inconsistent or suspicious account of how the injuries occurred.

When caring for a child who may have been abused, your first priority is to care for the child's illness or injuries. An abused child may be frightened, hysterical or withdrawn. He or she may be unwilling to talk about the incident in an attempt to protect the abuser. If you suspect abuse, explain your concerns to responding police officers or emergency medical services (EMS) personnel if possible.

If you think you have reasonable cause to believe that abuse has occurred, report your suspicions to a community or state agency, such as the Department of Social Services, the Department of Child and Family Services or Child Protective Services. You may be afraid to report suspected child abuse because you do not wish to get involved or are afraid of getting sued. However, in most states, when you make a report in good faith, you are immune from any civil or criminal liability or penalty, even if you made a mistake. In this instance, "good faith" means that you honestly believe that abuse has occurred or the potential for abuse exists, and a prudent and reasonable person in the same position would also honestly believe abuse has occurred or the potential for abuse exists. You do not need to identify yourself when you report child abuse, although your report will have more credibility if you do.

Sudden Infant Death Syndrome

Sudden infant death syndrome (SIDS) is a disorder that causes seemingly healthy infants to stop breathing while they sleep. SIDS is a leading cause of death for infants between 1 month and 1 year of age. By the time the infant's condition has been discovered, he or she will be in cardiac arrest. If you encounter an infant in this condition, make sure someone has called 9-1-1 or the local emergency number or call yourself. Perform cardiopulmonary resuscitation (CPR) on the infant until EMS personnel arrive.

An incident involving a severely injured or ill infant or child or one who has died can be emotionally upsetting. After such an episode, find someone you trust with whom you can talk about the experience and express your feelings. If you continue to be distressed, seek professional counseling. The feelings engendered by such incidents need to be dealt with and understood or they can result in serious stress reactions.

CARING FOR AN OLDER ADULT

Caring for an older adult requires that you keep in mind special problems and concerns. Often the problems seem unimportant to the older person. Often fear of loss of independence will cause an older adult to avoid treatment.

Remember the following when caring for an older adult:

- Do not talk down to an older adult, as you would a child.
- Falls are a common source of injury.
  - When an older adult person falls, always suspect head, neck, back or hip injuries.
- Realize that the signals or the seriousness of an injury may not occur for days. Therefore, persons close to the older person should be alert to signals of unusual behavior.
- The most important action you can take is to see that, if appropriate, the older adult is taken to a medical facility.

Physical and mental changes can occur as a result of aging. Because of these changes, many older adults are particularly susceptible to certain problems. These problems may require you to adapt your way of communicating and to be aware of certain potential age-related conditions.

Falls

As a result of slower reflexes, failing eyesight and hearing, arthritis and problems such as unsteady balance and movement, older adults are at increased risk of falls. Falls frequently result in fractures because the bones become weaker and more brittle with age.

Head Injuries

As we age, the size of our brains decreases. This decrease results in more space between the surface of the brain and the inside of the skull, which allows more movement of the brain within the skull, increasing the likelihood of serious head injury. Occasionally, an older adult may not develop the signals of a head injury until days after a fall. Therefore, unless you know the cause of a behavior change, you should always suspect a head injury as a possible cause of unusual behavior in an older adult, especially if the person has had a fall or a blow to the head.

Confusion

The older adult is at increased risk of altered thinking patterns and confusion. Some of this change is the result of aging. Certain diseases, such as Alzheimer's disease, affect the brain, resulting in impaired memory and thinking and altered behavior. Confusion that comes on suddenly, however, may be the result of medication, even a medication the person has been taking regularly. An ill or injured person who has problems seeing or hearing may also become confused when ill or injured. This problem increases when the person is in an unfamiliar environment. A head injury can also result in confusion.

Problems with Heat and Cold

An older adult is more susceptible to extremes in temperature. The person may be unable to feel temperature extremes because his or her body may no longer regulate temperature effectively. Body temperature may rapidly change to a dangerously high or low level.

PEOPLE WITH DISABILITIES

General hints for approaching an ill or injured person who you have reason to believe is disabled include—

- Speaking to the person before touching him or her.
- Asking "How can I help?" or "Do you need help?"
- Asking for assistance and information from the person who has the disability—he or

she has been living with the disability and best understands it. If the person is not able to communicate, ask family members, friends or companions who are available.

- Being sure to not remove any braces, canes, other physical support, eyeglasses or hearing aids. Removal of these items may take away necessary physical support for the person's body.
- Looking for a medical ID bracelet or necklace at the person's wrist or neck.
- Being aware that a person with a disability may have an animal assistant, such as a guide or hearing dog. This animal may be protective of the person in an emergency situation. Someone may need to calm and restrain the animal. Allow the animal to stay with the person if possible, which will help reassure them both.

LANGUAGE BARRIERS

One reason for an uncertain look when you speak to someone is that the person may not understand English or any other language you may speak. Getting consent to give care to a person with whom you have a language barrier can be a problem. Find out if any bystanders speak the person's language and can help translate. Do your best to communicate non-verbally. Use gestures and facial expressions. If the person is in pain, he or she will probably be anxious to let you know where that pain is. Watch his or her gestures and facial expressions carefully. Speak slowly and in a normal tone. The person probably will have no trouble hearing you. When you call 9-1-1 or the local emergency number, explain that you are having difficulty communicating with the person and say what nationality you believe he or she is or what language you believe he or she speaks. The EMS system may have someone available who can help with communication. If the person has a life-threatening condition, such as severe bleeding, consent is implied.

CARE FOR EMERGENCY CHILDBIRTH

If a woman is giving birth—
- Call 9-1-1 or the local emergency number.
- Give the EMS dispatcher the following important information:
  - The woman's name, age and expected due date
  - How long she has been having labor pains
  - If this is her first child
- Talk with the woman to help her stay calm.
- Place layers of newspaper covered with layers of linens, towels or blankets under her.
- Control the scene so that the woman will have privacy.
- Position her on her back with knees bent, feet flat and legs spread wide apart.
- Remember, the woman delivers the baby, so be patient and let it happen naturally.
- Keep the baby warm.

Cautions—
- *Do not let the woman get up or leave to find a bathroom (most women have a desire to use the restroom).*
- *Do not hold her knees together; this will not slow the birth process and may complicate the birth or harm the baby.*
- *Do not place your fingers in the vagina for any reason.*
- *Do not pull on the baby.*

ASTHMA

The instructions in this appendix are not a substitute for the directions that a medical professional gives to a person or gives as a consultation to a site where this equipment will be used. **Consult a health care professional for specific advice on use of this equipment.**

Asthma is an ongoing illness in which airways (small tubes in the lungs through which we breathe) have ongoing swelling. An asthma attack happens when a trigger, such as exercise, cold air, allergens or other irritants, affects the airways causing them to suddenly swell and narrow. This makes breathing difficult, which is frightening (Fig. G-1).

G-1

TRIGGERS OF AN ASTHMA ATTACK

A trigger is anything that sets off or starts an asthma attack. A trigger for one person is not necessarily a trigger for another. Some asthma triggers are—
- Dust, smoke and air pollution.
- Fear or anxiety.
- Hard exercise.
- Plants and molds.
- Perfume.
- Colds.
- Some medications, such as aspirin.
- Animals' fur or feathers.
- Temperature extremes or changes in the weather.

These are only a few of the things that can trigger asthma in some people.

Limiting Triggers in the Home
You can reduce the chances of triggering an asthma attack at home by—
- Keeping plants outside.
- Washing bedclothes weekly in hot water.
- Using hypoallergenic covers on mattresses and pillows.
- Eliminating or reducing the number of carpets and rugs.
- Regularly steam cleaning all carpets, rugs and upholstery.
- Keeping the home clean and free of dust and pests—wet dusting can be more effective than dry dusting.
- Not allowing, or being around, smoking.
- Changing the air filter in the central air or heating unit regularly.
- Eliminating or minimizing the number of stuffed toys.
- Using hypoallergenic health and beauty products.
- Washing pets weekly.
- Keeping pets outside the house.

SIGNALS OF AN ASTHMA ATTACK
- Coughing or wheezing
- Trouble breathing
- Shortness of breath
- Rapid shallow breathing
- Inability to talk without stopping for a breath
- Tightness in the chest
- Feelings of fear or confusion
- Sweating

MEDICATIONS

Some anti-inflammatory medications prescribed for the long-term control of asthma are taken daily (Fig. G-2). Other medications are prescribed for quick relief and are taken only when a person is experiencing the signals of an asthma attack. These medications help relieve the sudden swelling and are called bronchodilators (inhalers) (Fig. G-3).

G-2

G-3

SKILL SHEET: CARE FOR AN ASTHMA ATTACK

Remember: Always obtain consent, and wash your hands immediately after giving care.

CHECK the scene and the person; **CALL** 9-1-1 or the local emergency number if the breathing difficulty does not improve in a few minutes or worsens.

TO CARE for the person—

STEP 1: Help the person sit up and rest in a position comfortable for breathing.

STEP 2: If the person has medication for asthma, help him or her take it.

- **Ensure that the prescription is in the person's name and is prescribed for "quick relief" or "acute" attacks.** (Note: some inhalers contain long-acting, preventive medication that should NOT be used in the event of an emergency.)
- **Ensure that the expiration date of the medication has not passed** (Fig. G-4).

G-4

- **Read and follow any instructions** printed on the inhaler prior to administering the medication to the person.
- Note: Some inhalers have extension or spacer tubes that fit between the mouthpiece and the medication canister. If present, attach and utilize.

STEP 3: Shake the inhaler.

STEP 4: Remove the cover from the inhaler mouthpiece. (Some inhalers have extension or spacer tubes that fit between the mouthpiece and the medication canister. If present, attach and use) (Fig. G-5).

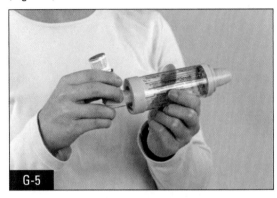

G-5

- **Tell the person to breathe out as much as possible.**

STEP 5: Have the person place his or her lips tightly around the mouthpiece. (Note: The person may use different techniques.)

STEP 6: As the person breathes in slowly, **administer the medication** (Fig. G-6) **by quickly pressing down on the inhaler canister** or the person may self-administer the medication (Fig. G-7).

- The person should continue to take a full, deep breath.
- Tell the person to try to hold his or her breath for a count of 10.
  - When using an extension tube, have the person take 5 or 6 deep breaths through the tube without holding his or her breath.

- **Note the time of administration and any change in the person's condition.**
- The medication may be repeated once after 1 minute.
  - Note: The medication may be repeated every 5 to 10 minutes thereafter, as needed, for areas with long emergency medical services response times such as rural locations.
    - These medications may take 5 to 15 minutes to reach full effectiveness.

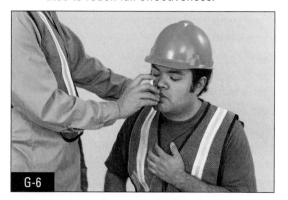

STEP 7: Stay with the person and monitor his or her condition. Have the person rinse his or her mouth out with water (Fig. G-8).

STEP 8: Care for shock. Keep the person from getting chilled or overheated.

EPINEPHRINE AUTO-INJECTOR

The instructions in this module are not a substitute for the directions that a medical professional gives to a person or gives as a consultation to a site where this equipment will be used. **Consult a health care professional for specific advice on use of this equipment.**

ANAPHYLAXIS

Every year in the United States, between 400 and 800 deaths are caused by severe allergic reactions. These reactions bring on a condition called *anaphylactic shock,* also known as *anaphylaxis.*

A person can die from anaphylaxis within just 1 minute of being exposed to an *antigen*—a foreign substance that brings on the allergic reaction. Fortunately, some deaths can be prevented if anaphylaxis is recognized early and cared for quickly.

ALLERGIC REACTIONS

Allergic reactions are caused by the activity of the immune system. The body recognizes and protects itself from antigens by producing *antibodies,* which fight antigens. Antibodies are found in the liver, bone marrow, spleen and lymph glands. The *immune system* recognizes the antigens and releases chemicals to fight these foreign substances and eliminate them from the body.

These reactions range from mild to very severe; for instance, the common mild reaction to poison ivy (skin irritation) to a life-threatening reaction (swelling of the airway, trouble breathing and obstructed airway).

Some common antigens include but may not be limited to bee or insect venom; antibiotics; pollen; animal dander; sulfa; and some foods such as nuts, peanuts, shellfish, strawberries and coconut oils.

SIGNALS OF ANAPHYLAXIS

Allergic reactions usually occur suddenly, within seconds or minutes after contact with the substance.

The skin or area that came in contact with the substance usually swells and turns red. Other signals may include—

- Hives, itching or rash.
- Weakness, nausea, vomiting or stomach cramps.
- Dizziness.
- Trouble breathing, including coughing and wheezing.
- Low blood pressure.
- Shock.

Trouble breathing can lead to an obstructed airway as the lips, tongue, throat and larynx (voice box) swell.

CARE FOR ANAPHYLAXIS

If you notice an unusual inflammation or rash on a person's skin just after he or she has come into contact with a possible antigen, the person may be having an allergic reaction, which can develop into anaphylaxis (Fig. H-1). If you suspect an allergic reaction—

- Check the person's airway, breathing and signs of circulation (**ABCs**).
- Call 9-1-1 or the local emergency number immediately if the person is having trouble breathing or if the person complains that his or her throat is closing.
- Help the person into the most comfortable position for breathing.
- Monitor the person's **ABCs** and try to keep the person calm.

H-1

People who know they are extremely allergic to certain substances usually try to avoid them, although this is sometimes impossible. These people may carry an anaphylaxis kit in case they have a severe reaction. Such kits, which are available by prescription only, can come in one- or two-dose units of the drug *epinephrine* that can be injected into the body to counteract the anaphylactic reaction. Many kits also contain an *antihistamine*, a substance that reduces the effects of compounds released by the body in allergic reactions, in a pill form.

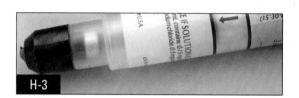

Images Courtesy of Dey, L.P.

Auto-Injectors

An auto-injector contains a preloaded dose of 0.3 mg of epinephrine for adults or 0.15 mg of epinephrine for children (Fig. H-2, A-B). The injector has a spring-loaded plunger that when activated injects the epinephrine. Forcefully pushing the auto-injector against the skin activates the device. It should be used on a person's upper arm or thigh in the muscular area. This injector needs to stay in place for 10 seconds to allow the medication to fully empty (Fig. H-3).

If a person is conscious and able to use the auto-injector, help him or her in any way asked. Call 9-1-1 or the local emergency number. If someone reacts so severely to a specific antigen that a physician has prescribed an epinephrine auto-injector, then the person might need advanced medical care and time is of the essence. If you know that a person has a prescribed auto-injector and is unable to administer it him or herself, then you may help the person use it.

Needlestick Safety and Prevention Act

Blood and other potentially infectious materials have long been recognized as a potential threat to the health of employees who are exposed to these materials through penetration of the skin. Injuries from contaminated needles and other sharps have been associated with an increased risk of disease from more than 20 infectious agents. The most serious pathogens are human immunodeficiency virus, hepatitis B virus and hepatitis C virus. Needlesticks and other sharps injuries resulting in exposure to blood or other potentially infectious materials are a concern because they happen frequently and can have serious health effects.

For information on the Needlestick Safety and Prevention Act, visit Occupational Safety and Health Administration's Web site at **www.osha.gov/pls/oshaweb/owadisp.show_document?p_table=FEDERAL_REGISTER&p_id=16265**.

SKILL SHEET: EPINEPHRINE AUTO-INJECTOR

BEFORE ASSISTING WITH AN AUTO-INJECTOR

STEP 1: CHECK the scene and the person.

STEP 2: Obtain consent.

STEP 3: If the person is unconscious, has trouble breathing, complains that his or her throat is tightening or explains that he or she is subject to severe allergic reactions, have someone **CALL 9-1-1** or the local emergency number.

STEP 4: If the person is conscious and can talk, ask—
- What is your name?
- What happened?
- How do you feel?
- Do you feel any tingling in your hands, feet or lips?
- Do you feel pain anywhere?
- Do you have any allergies? Do you have prescribed medications to take in case of an allergic reaction?
- Do you know what triggered the reaction?
- How much and how long were you exposed?
- Do you have any medical conditions or are you taking any medications?

STEP 5: Check the person from head to toe—
- Observe for signals of respiratory distress or allergic reactions.
- Look for a medical ID bracelet.

STEPS FOR ASSISTING WITH AN AUTO-INJECTOR

Determine whether the person has already taken epinephrine or antihistamine. If so, DO NOT ADMINISTER ANOTHER DOSE unless directed by EMS.

Check the label to confirm that the prescription of the auto-injector is for this person (Fig. H-4).

H-4

Check the expiration date of the auto-injector. If it has expired, DO NOT USE IT. If the medication is visible, confirm that the liquid is clear and not cloudy. If it is cloudy, DO NOT USE IT.

AFTER CHECKING A CONSCIOUS PERSON—

STEP 1: Locate the middle of one thigh or the upper arm to use as the injection site (Fig. H-5).

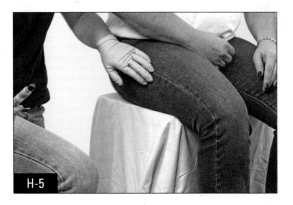

H-5

Grasp the auto-injector firmly in your fist and pull off the safety cap with your other hand (Fig. H-6).

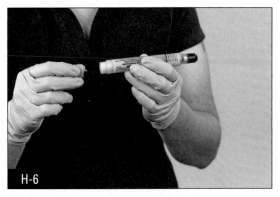

STEP 2: Hold the (black) tip (needle end) near the person's outer thigh so that the auto-injector is at a 90-degree angle to the thigh (Fig. H-7).

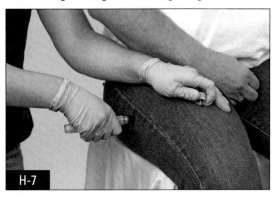

STEP 3: Swing out then firmly jab the tip straight into the outer thigh. You will hear a click.

Note: If possible, help the person self-administer the auto-injector (Fig. H-8).

STEP 4: Hold the auto-injector firmly in place for 10 seconds, then remove it from the thigh and massage the injection site for several seconds (Fig. H-9).

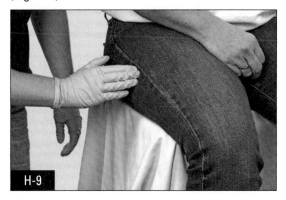

Note: Recheck the person's airway, breathing and circulation and observe his or her response to the epinephrine.

STEP 5: Give the used auto-injector to the emergency medical services personnel when they arrive (Fig. H-10).

EXAMS AND ANSWER SHEETS

- American Red Cross Before Giving Care Exam A

- American Red Cross CPR Component Exam A

- American Red Cross AED Component Exam A

- American Red Cross First Aid Component Exam A

- Answer Sheets

AMERICAN RED CROSS

IMPORTANT: Read all instructions before beginning the exam.

INSTRUCTIONS: Mark all answers in pencil on the separate answer sheet as directed by your instructor. Do not write on this exam. Read each question slowly and carefully. Then choose the best answer and fill in that circle on the answer sheet. If you wish to change an answer, erase your first answer completely. Return this exam with your answer sheet to your instructor when you are finished.

EXAMPLE

xx. **Why does the American Red Cross teach this course?**
a. To help people stay calm in emergencies.
b. To help people make appropriate decisions when they confront an emergency.
c. To help people in an emergency keep a victim's injuries from getting worse until EMS arrives.
d. All of the above.

ANSWER SHEET

XX.   ⓐ   ⓑ   ⓒ   ●

Exam A   Before Giving Care

1. What type of signals may help you notice an emergency?
a. Unusual noises.
b. Unusual odors.
c. Unusual appearances or behaviors.
d. All of the above.

2. What should you do if the person does not give consent?
a. Give care and call 9-1-1 or the local emergency number.
b. Give care and do not call 9-1-1 or the local emergency number.
c. Do not give care but do call 9-1-1 or the local emergency number.
d. None of the above.

3. The steps to follow in an emergency are—
a. Call—Check—Secure.
b. Check—Care—Defibrillate.
c. Check—Call—Care.
d. Care—Call—Check.

4. When should you call 9-1-1 or the local emergency number?
a. The person has a cough and runny nose.
b. The person has a stomachache that goes away.
c. The person has an earache.
d. The person has trouble breathing.

5. Move an injured person *only* if—
   a. The scene is or is becoming unsafe.
   b. You need to reach another person with more serious injury or illness.
   c. You need to move a person to give emergency care.
   d. All of the above.

6. By following standard precautions to protect yourself and the person, you can—
   a. Minimize the risk of disease transmission.
   b. Reduce the number of times you need to wear gloves.
   c. Increase the risk of disease transmission.
   d. None of the above.

7. How should you check a conscious person?
   a. Get consent to give care.
   b. Ask questions.
   c. Do not touch or move painful, injured areas on the body.
   d. All of the above.

8. You determine that a person may be in shock. Do each of the following *except*—
   a. Keep the person comfortable.
   b. Give the person water.
   c. Monitor the person's ABCs.
   d. Raise the person's legs 12 inches.

9. The best way to check if a person is unconscious is to—
   a. Lift the person up.
   b. Give the person CPR.
   c. Tap the person and shout, "Are you okay?"
   d. Look, listen and feel for signs of breathing.

10. You see a woman collapse in front of you while entering the lobby of your office building. You check the scene and then check the victim for consciousness, but she does not respond. What should you do next?
    a. Call or have someone else call EMS.
    b. Check for signs of life.
    c. Drive the person to the hospital.
    d. Give 2 rescue breaths.

1. **Which of the following are signals of trouble breathing?**
   a. Noisy or painful breathing.
   b. Unusually deep or shallow breathing.
   c. Changes in skin color.
   d. All of the above.

2. **What care should you give to a conscious adult who is choking and cannot cough, speak or breathe?**
   a. Give 2 slow rescue breaths.
   b. Do a foreign object look/removal.
   c. Give back blows and abdominal thrusts.
   d. Lower the person to the floor and open the airway.

3. **Always check for signs of life for no more than—**
   a. 1 second.
   b. 2 seconds.
   c. 5 seconds.
   d. 10 seconds.

4. **When giving a rescue breath to an adult, you should give the breath over a period of about—**
   a. 1 second.
   b. ½ second.
   c. 3 seconds.
   d. 4 seconds.

5. **If a person is suffering from pain or discomfort in the chest that lasts more than 3 to 5 minutes or that goes away and comes back, this person is most likely having—**
   a. A heat-related emergency.
   b. A cold-related emergency.
   c. A heart attack.
   d. A seizure.

6. **About how many cycles of CPR should you perform for an adult in 2 minutes?**
   a. 2
   b. 4
   c. 5
   d. 1

7. **The cycle of compressions and breaths in CPR for an adult is—**
   a. 15 compressions for every 3 breaths.
   b. 15 compressions for every 1 breath.
   c. 30 compressions for every 2 breaths.
   d. 30 compressions for every 1 breath.

8. **About how often should you stop and check for signs of life when performing CPR on an adult?**
   a. After the first minute, then every other minute thereafter.
   b. CPR should not be interrupted or stopped until an AED is ready to use, another trained responder takes over or you see an obvious sign of life.
   c. After every minute (or after every 4 cycles of compressions and breaths).
   d. After the first minute, then not again until EMS personnel arrive.

9. **Early CPR is an important link in the Cardiac Chain of Survival because—**
   a. CPR prevents heart attacks.
   b. With early CPR, most cardiac arrest victims do not need defibrillation.
   c. It helps circulate blood that contains oxygen to the vital organs until an AED is ready to use or advanced medical personnel arrive.
   d. It helps restart the heart.

10. **You should continue CPR until—**
    a. The scene is determined to be safe.
    b. The person's condition worsens.
    c. You are too exhausted to continue.
    d. You need to call 9-1-1 or the local emergency number for advice on a nonlife-threatening condition.

1. **Which of the following are signals of trouble breathing?**
   a. Agitation.
   b. Slow or rapid breathing.
   c. Pale, ashen, flushed or bluish skin color.
   d. All of the above.

2. **A child is choking on a piece of hard candy. She is conscious and coughing forcefully. What should you do?**
   a. Lay her down and give abdominal thrusts.
   b. Stay with her and encourage her to continue coughing.
   c. Do a foreign object look/removal.
   d. Slap her on the back until she stops coughing.

3. **When giving rescue breaths to a child, how should you breathe into the child?**
   a. As fast as you can.
   b. Give a breath over a period of about 1 second.
   c. As hard as you can.
   d. a and c.

4. **Performing early CPR on a child in cardiac arrest can—**
   a. Reduce the child's need for oxygen.
   b. Keep vital organs supplied with blood containing oxygen.
   c. Cause permanent brain damage.
   d. None of the above.

5. **When giving CPR—**
   a. Compress the chest straight down about 1 to 1 ½ inches.
   b. Give cycles of 30 chest compressions and 2 rescue breaths.
   c. Compress the chest at a 45-degree angle.
   d. a and b.

6. **When giving rescue breaths to a child, you should give 1 breath about every—**
   a. 5 seconds.
   b. 3 seconds.
   c. 9 seconds.
   d. 15 seconds.

7. **You notice that a child looks panicked and cannot cough, speak or breathe. What life-threatening condition could the child be experiencing?**
   a. Indigestion.
   b. Cardiac arrest.
   c. Upset stomach.
   d. Choking.

8. **The cycle of compressions and breaths in CPR for a child is—**
   a. 15 compressions for every 3 breaths.
   b. 15 compressions for every 1 breath.
   c. 30 compressions for every 2 breaths.
   d. 30 compressions for every 1 breath.

9. **When giving care to a child who is conscious and has an obstructed airway, where should you position your fist to give abdominal thrusts?**
   a. On the rib cage.
   b. In the center of the breastbone.
   c. Just above the navel.
   d. Any of the above.

10. **About how often should you stop and check for signs of life when performing rescue breathing on a child?**
    a. After the first minute, then every 30 seconds thereafter.
    b. After every 2 minutes (or 40 breaths).
    c. After every minute.
    d. After the first minute, then not again until EMS personnel arrive.

1. **Some signals that indicate an infant is choking are—**
   a. Rapid breathing and crying.
   b. Looking panicked and not able to cough, cry or breathe.
   c. Breathing noisily and deeply.
   d. Crying and spitting up food.

2. **About how often should you stop and check for breathing and a pulse when performing rescue breathing on an infant?**
   a. About every 2 minutes (or 40 breaths).
   b. After the first minute, then every 30 seconds thereafter.
   c. After every minute.
   d. After the first minute, then not again until EMS personnel arrive.

3. **When giving rescue breaths to an infant, you should give 1 breath about every—**
   a. 5 seconds.
   b. 3 seconds.
   c. 9 seconds.
   d. 15 seconds.

4. **The cycle of compressions and breaths in CPR for an infant is—**
   a. 15 compressions for every 3 breaths.
   b. 30 compressions for every 2 breaths.
   c. 15 compressions for every 1 breath.
   d. 30 compressions for every 1 breath.

5. **Where should you place your hands when compressing an infant's chest during CPR?**
   a. One hand on the chin and one hand on the chest.
   b. One hand on the forehead and one hand on the chest.
   c. One hand on the chin and 2 or 3 fingers on the center of the chest.
   d. One hand on the infant's forehead and 2 or 3 fingers on the center of the chest.

6. **What should you do for a conscious infant who is choking and cannot cough, cry or breathe?**
   a. Give abdominal thrusts.
   b. Give back blows until the infant starts to cough.
   c. Give back blows and chest thrusts to clear the airway.
   d. Any of the above will probably clear the airway.

7. **One signal of a breathing emergency in an infant is—**
   a. Being awake and alert.
   b. Breathing calmly and quietly.
   c. Making a wheezing or high-pitched sound.
   d. Sleeping with calm breathing.

8. An infant in need of CPR will show—
   a. Rapid and shallow breathing.
   b. No breathing and no pulse.
   c. Signs of life and will be conscious.
   d. Breathing and no other signs of life.

9. When giving CPR to an infant—
   a. Compress the chest straight down about $\frac{1}{2}$ to 1 inch.
   b. Give cycles of 30 chest compressions and 2 rescue breaths.
   c. Compress the chest at a 45-degree angle.
   d. Both a and b.

10. Where should you position a conscious choking infant's head?
    a. In the head-tilt/chin-lift position.
    b. With the infant's head lower than his or her chest.
    c. Flat and face-down on your leg or a table.
    d. In a sitting position with the infant's head higher than his or her chest.

1. **Each minute that defibrillation is delayed reduces the chance of survival of a sudden cardiac arrest victim by about—**
   a. 3 percent.
   b. 50 percent.
   c. 10 percent.
   d. 40 percent.

2. **Early defibrillation can—**
   a. Result in more effective CPR.
   b. Eliminate the need for advanced medical care.
   c. Help recognize when a person is not breathing.
   d. Save the lives of more people in cardiac arrest.

3. **Which of the following statements about defibrillation is true?**
   a. It is more likely to be successful if CPR is withheld.
   b. It can be used to restart a heart without any electrical activity.
   c. It is an electric shock that may help the heart to resume an effective rhythm to a person in sudden cardiac arrest.
   d. It is commonly used on a person complaining of chest pain.

4. **If, during the second analysis, the AED prompts "no shock advised," you should—**
   a. Unplug the connector from the machine.
   b. Resume 5 cycles or about 2 minutes of CPR.
   c. Reset the AED by turning it off for 10 seconds.
   d. Check the pad placement on the person's chest.

5. **What should you do before the AED analyzes the rhythm?**
   a. Ensure that no one, including you, is touching the person.
   b. Ensure that the head tilt/jaw thrust is maintained.
   c. Ensure that the person shows signs of life and is breathing.
   d. None of the above.

6. **When preparing an AED for use, what is the *first* thing you should do?**
   a. Turn on the AED.
   b. Deliver a shock.
   c. Stand clear.
   d. Begin 1 ½ minutes of CPR.

7. **Why is it important to stand clear and not touch the person before delivering a shock with an AED?**
   a. The AED may not deliver enough electrical energy.
   b. You or someone else could be injured by the shock.
   c. You might prevent the AED from analyzing the heart rhythm properly.
   d. All of the above.

8. **If, prior to applying the pads, you see a medication patch on the person's chest you should—**
   a. With a gloved hand, remove the patch from the person's chest.
   b. Leave the patch attached to the person and do not touch it.
   c. Move the patch to another spot on the person.
   d. Remove the patch using your bare hand and throw it away.

9. **The AED pads for an adult should be placed on—**
   a. The upper left and the lower right side of the chest.
   b. The upper right and the upper left side of the chest.
   c. The chest and stomach of the person's torso.
   d. The upper right and the lower left side of the chest.

10. **Once you have attached AED pads to a person, you should—**
   a. Give abdominal thrusts.
   b. Allow or activate the AED to analyze the heart rhythm.
   c. Check for signs of life.
   d. Give chest compressions.

1. **Why is it important to stand clear and not touch the child before analyzing the heart rhythm or delivering a shock?**
   a. The AED will turn off.
   b. You or someone else could become injured by the shock.
   c. You may prevent the AED from analyzing the heart rhythm properly.
   d. Both b and c.

2. **Before delivering a shock with an AED to a child, you should—**
   a. Look for a foreign object in the child's mouth.
   b. Place the child on his or her side.
   c. Have another responder hold the child.
   d. Ensure that no one, including you, is touching or is in contact with the child.

3. **Causes of cardiac arrest in children include—**
   a. Traumatic injuries or accidents.
   b. Breathing emergencies.
   c. A hard blow to the chest.
   d. All of the above.

4. **A responder who is alone and witnesses a child who suddenly collapses in cardiac arrest should—**
   a. Give 5 minutes of CPR before taking other actions, such as calling 9-1-1 or the local emergency number.
   b. Give rescue breathing only.
   c. Call for help first.
   d. Give 7 minutes of CPR and then call for help.

5. **The pediatric AED pads for a child can be placed on—**
   a. The upper left and the lower right side of the child's chest.
   b. The upper right and the lower left side of the child's chest.
   c. The child's upper right arm and the left side of his or her chest.
   d. None of the above.

6. **Which of the following precautions apply when operating an AED?**
   a. Do not use an AED on a child lying in water.
   b. Do not touch the child when defibrillating.
   c. Do not touch the child while the AED is analyzing.
   d. All of the above.

7. **What should you do if the pediatric AED pads risk touching each other when placed on a smaller child's chest?**
   a. Place one pad on the child's chest and the other on the child's back.
   b. Leave them as they are—it does not matter if they touch.
   c. Use adult AED pads.
   d. Use just one pad.

8. **If, after giving 1 shock, the AED prompts "No shock advised," you should—**
   a. Immediately reanalyze the rhythm.
   b. Resume 5 cycles or about 2 minutes of CPR.
   c. Reset the AED by turning it off for 10 seconds.
   d. Check the pad placement on the child's chest.

9. **You have just responded with an AED to an emergency involving a 7-year-old child. You check the child and find no signs of life. What should you do *first* to prepare the AED for use?**
   a. Turn on the AED.
   b. Deliver a shock.
   c. Stand clear.
   d. Give 5 minutes of CPR.

10. **Which of the following statements about defibrillation is true?**
   a. It is more likely to be successful if CPR is withheld.
   b. It can be used to restart a heart without any electrical activity.
   c. It is an electric shock that may help the heart to resume an effective rhythm to a child in cardiac arrest.
   d. It is commonly used on a child complaining of chest pain.

1. **A woman burned her hand in the lunchroom. You should—**
   a. Stop the burning.
   b. Cool the burn with large amounts of cold water.
   c. Cover the burn loosely with a dry, sterile dressing.
   d. All of the above.

2. **Which type of injury involves an open wound where the bone has torn through the skin?**
   a. Sprain.
   b. Dislocation.
   c. Strain.
   d. Open fracture.

3. **In general, a splint should be—**
   a. Snug, but not so tight that it slows circulation.
   b. Loose, so the person can still move the injured limb.
   c. Tied with cravats over the injured area.
   d. None of the above.

4. **When caring for a person who is having a seizure, you should—**
   a. Try to hold the person still.
   b. Remove nearby objects that might cause injury.
   c. Place a spoon or wallet between the person's teeth.
   d. All of the above.

5. **What sudden illness is usually caused by a blockage of blood flow to the brain?**
   a. Heat-related illness.
   b. Heart attack.
   c. Diabetic emergency.
   d. Stroke.

6. **This sudden illness results from too much or too little sugar in the person's blood. What is it?**
   a. Stroke.
   b. Diabetic emergency.
   c. Seizure.
   d. Allergic reaction.

7. **What should you do for a person with heat exhaustion?**
   a. Force the person to quickly drink a lot of water.
   b. Get the person out of the heat and into a cooler place.
   c. Put more layers of clothing on the person as a protection against the heat.
   d. All of the above.

8. The progression that heat-related emergencies can follow from early stage (least severe) to late stage (most severe) is—
   a. Heat cramps, heat stroke, heat exhaustion.
   b. Heat exhaustion, heat stroke, heat cramps.
   c. Heat cramps, heat exhaustion, heat stroke.
   d. Heat exhaustion, heat cramps, heat stroke.

9. How should you care for someone with frostbitten hands?
   a. Immerse his or her hands in hot water.
   b. Massage his or her hands vigorously.
   c. Have the person shake his or her hands vigorously until feeling is restored.
   d. Get the person to a warm environment and then rewarm his or her hands in warm water.

10. What is the *first* step in caring for a bleeding wound?
    a. Apply pressure at a pressure point.
    b. Add bulky dressing to reinforce blood-soaked bandages.
    c. Apply direct pressure with a sterile or clean dressing.
    d. Care for shock.

11. What signals can you look for to determine if a person is bleeding internally?
    a. The person is vomiting blood or coughing up blood.
    b. There are tender, swollen, bruised areas or hard bumps on the body.
    c. The person is becoming confused, faint, drowsy or unconscious.
    d. All of the above.

12. How should you care for a person with a possible head, neck or back injury?
    a. Move the person into a comfortable position as soon as possible.
    b. Move the injured area so that it rests above the person's heart.
    c. Minimize movement of the head, neck and back.
    d. None of the above.

13. In stroke recognition, F.A.S.T. means—
    a. Face, arm, speech and time.
    b. Feet, airway, speech and temperature.
    c. Fever, anxiety, stress and taste.
    d. Flexibility, asthma, sudden tightness in the chest.

14. **You suspect that someone is having a severe allergic reaction to a bee sting and is having trouble breathing. What should you do?**
   a. Give the person abdominal thrusts.
   b. After about 15 minutes call 9-1-1.
   c. Call 9-1-1 immediately and care for the person until help arrives.
   d. Give the person a cool drink.

15. **What should you do if you suspect that a conscious person has been poisoned?**
   a. Call the local pharmacy.
   b. Call the Poison Control Center and follow the advice given.
   c. Give the person large amounts of milk.
   d. Immediately induce vomiting.

ANSWER SHEET: FIRST AID/CPR/AED—CPR COMPONENT

Name: _____   **Date:** _____

DIRECTIONS: Beside the number of each question, fill in with a pencil the circle containing the letter of your answer. Return the exam and answer sheet to your instructor when you are finished.

Exam (A) (B) Before Giving Care

1. (a) (b) (c) (d)
2. (a) (b) (c) (d)
3. (a) (b) (c) (d)
4. (a) (b) (c) (d)
5. (a) (b) (c) (d)
6. (a) (b) (c) (d)
7. (a) (b) (c) (d)
8. (a) (b) (c) (d)
9. (a) (b) (c) (d)
10. (a) (b) (c) (d)

Exam (A) (B) CPR—Child

1. (a) (b) (c) (d)
2. (a) (b) (c) (d)
3. (a) (b) (c) (d)
4. (a) (b) (c) (d)
5. (a) (b) (c) (d)
6. (a) (b) (c) (d)
7. (a) (b) (c) (d)
8. (a) (b) (c) (d)
9. (a) (b) (c) (d)
10. (a) (b) (c) (d)

Exam (A) (B) CPR—Adult

1. (a) (b) (c) (d)
2. (a) (b) (c) (d)
3. (a) (b) (c) (d)
4. (a) (b) (c) (d)
5. (a) (b) (c) (d)
6. (a) (b) (c) (d)
7. (a) (b) (c) (d)
8. (a) (b) (c) (d)
9. (a) (b) (c) (d)
10. (a) (b) (c) (d)

Exam (A) (B) CPR—Infant

1. (a) (b) (c) (d)
2. (a) (b) (c) (d)
3. (a) (b) (c) (d)
4. (a) (b) (c) (d)
5. (a) (b) (c) (d)
6. (a) (b) (c) (d)
7. (a) (b) (c) (d)
8. (a) (b) (c) (d)
9. (a) (b) (c) (d)
10. (a) (b) (c) (d)

ANSWER SHEET: FIRST AID/CPR/AED—AED AND FIRST AID COMPONENTS

Name: _____ **Date:** _____

DIRECTIONS: Beside the number of each question, fill in with a pencil the circle containing the letter of your answer. Return the exam and answer sheet to your instructor when you are finished.

Exam Ⓐ Ⓑ AED—Adult

1.	ⓐ	ⓑ	ⓒ	ⓓ
2.	ⓐ	ⓑ	ⓒ	ⓓ
3.	ⓐ	ⓑ	ⓒ	ⓓ
4.	ⓐ	ⓑ	ⓒ	ⓓ
5.	ⓐ	ⓑ	ⓒ	ⓓ
6.	ⓐ	ⓑ	ⓒ	ⓓ
7.	ⓐ	ⓑ	ⓒ	ⓓ
8.	ⓐ	ⓑ	ⓒ	ⓓ
9.	ⓐ	ⓑ	ⓒ	ⓓ
10.	ⓐ	ⓑ	ⓒ	ⓓ

Exam Ⓐ Ⓑ AED—Child

1.	ⓐ	ⓑ	ⓒ	ⓓ
2.	ⓐ	ⓑ	ⓒ	ⓓ
3.	ⓐ	ⓑ	ⓒ	ⓓ
4.	ⓐ	ⓑ	ⓒ	ⓓ
5.	ⓐ	ⓑ	ⓒ	ⓓ
6.	ⓐ	ⓑ	ⓒ	ⓓ
7.	ⓐ	ⓑ	ⓒ	ⓓ
8.	ⓐ	ⓑ	ⓒ	ⓓ
9.	ⓐ	ⓑ	ⓒ	ⓓ
10.	ⓐ	ⓑ	ⓒ	ⓓ

Exam Ⓐ Ⓑ First Aid

1.	ⓐ	ⓑ	ⓒ	ⓓ		11.	ⓐ	ⓑ	ⓒ	ⓓ
2.	ⓐ	ⓑ	ⓒ	ⓓ		12.	ⓐ	ⓑ	ⓒ	ⓓ
3.	ⓐ	ⓑ	ⓒ	ⓓ		13.	ⓐ	ⓑ	ⓒ	ⓓ
4.	ⓐ	ⓑ	ⓒ	ⓓ		14.	ⓐ	ⓑ	ⓒ	ⓓ
5.	ⓐ	ⓑ	ⓒ	ⓓ		15.	ⓐ	ⓑ	ⓒ	ⓓ
6.	ⓐ	ⓑ	ⓒ	ⓓ						
7.	ⓐ	ⓑ	ⓒ	ⓓ						
8.	ⓐ	ⓑ	ⓒ	ⓓ						
9.	ⓐ	ⓑ	ⓒ	ⓓ						
10.	ⓐ	ⓑ	ⓒ	ⓓ						

Josie.

866-252-4511